Governance: A Very Short Introduction

VERY SHORT INTRODUCTIONS are for anyone wanting a stimulating and accessible way into a new subject. They are written by experts, and have been translated into more than 45 different languages.

The series began in 1995, and now covers a wide variety of topics in every discipline. The VSI library now contains over 500 volumes—a Very Short Introduction to everything from Psychology and Philosophy of Science to American History and Relativity—and continues to grow in every subject area.

Titles in the series include the following:

Mark Bevir

GOVERNANCE

A Very Short Introduction

OXFORD
UNIVERSITY PRESS

OXFORD
UNIVERSITY PRESS

Great Clarendon Street, Oxford, OX2 6DP,
United Kingdom

Oxford University Press is a department of the University of Oxford.
It furthers the University's objective of excellence in research, scholarship,
and education by publishing worldwide. Oxford is a registered trade mark of
Oxford University Press in the UK and in certain other countries

First Edition published in 2012

Impression: 14

British Library Cataloguing in Publication Data
Data available

Library of Congress Cataloging in Publication Data
Data available

ISBN 978-0-19-960641-2

Printed in Great Britain by
Ashford Colour Press Ltd., Gosport, Hampshire.

Contents

Contents

List of illustrations

List of Abbreviations

CEO	Chief Executive Officer
CSR	Corporate Social Responsibility
EU	European Union
ICBL	International Campaign to Ban Landmines
MSC	Marine Stewardship Council
NGO	non-governmental organization
OECD	Organization for Economic Cooperation and Development
PPP	Public–Private Partnership
UN	United Nations
UNSC	United Nations Security Council
WWF	World Wildlife Fund

Chapter 1
What is governance?

Since the 1980s the word 'governance' has become ubiquitous. Newspapers bemoan crumbling standards of corporate governance. The European Union issues White Papers on Governance. Climate change and avian flu appear as issues of global governance. The US Forest Service calls for greater collaborative governance. What accounts for the rapid spread of the word 'governance'? To what does governance refer? How does governance differ from government? In brief, governance has spread rapidly both because changing social theories have led people to see the world differently and because the world itself has changed. New theories and practices have drawn attention away from the central institutions of the state and towards the activity of governing, and much of the activity of governing now involves private and voluntary organizations as well as public ones. Governance refers, therefore, to all processes of governing, whether undertaken by a government, market, or network, whether over a family, tribe, formal or informal organization, or territory, and whether through laws, norms, power, or language. Governance differs from government in that it focuses less on the state and its institutions and more on social practices and activities. To understand governance requires that we look at abstract theories of hierarchy, market, and network as types of organizations, and then at more concrete debates about the shift from hierarchy to markets and networks in corporations, the public sector, and global politics.

Governance and government

A first task is to show that governance is a coherent concept that does useful work. Some sceptics think governance is merely jargon. 'Governance' might appear to be a weasel word—a vague euphemism for government. Other sceptics believe that the word 'governance' is used so widely that it has become tired. Discussions of governance occur in diverse contexts and disciplines, including development studies, economics, geography, international relations, planning, political science, public administration, and sociology. Too little attention is given to ways of making sense of the whole literature on governance.

Governance differs from government both theoretically and empirically. In theoretical terms, governance is the process of governing. It is what governments do to their citizens. But it is also what corporations and other organizations do to their employees and members. Further, the process of governing need

1. The term 'governance' draws attention to processes of decision-making and ruling throughout society including, for example, this board of governors meeting in a British school

not be consciously undertaken by a hierarchically organized set of actors. Markets and networks of actors can govern, produce coordination, and make decisions. Whereas government refers to political institutions, governance refers to processes of rule wherever they occur.

In empirical terms, governance refers to a shift in public organization since the 1980s. The world of government has changed. Increasingly governments rely on private and voluntary sector actors to manage and deliver services. The state enters contracts with other organizations, for example, to manage prisons and to provide training to the unemployed. The state forms partnerships with other organizations, for example, to build roads and rail lines and to deliver humanitarian aid. Whereas government had consisted in no small measure of bureaucratic hierarchies, the new governance gives greater scope to markets and networks.

Governance has abstract theoretical and concrete empirical uses. As an abstract theoretical concept, governance refers to all processes of social organization and social coordination. Governance here differs from government because social organization need not involve oversight and control, let alone the state. Markets and networks might provide governance in the absence of any significant government. This abstract use of the word 'governance' provides a language with which to discuss general theoretical questions about the nature of society, organization, and coordination.

The more concrete empirical uses of governance refer to changing organizational practices within corporations, the public sector, and the global order. Although debates surround the extent of the new governance and also the role of the state in it, there is a widespread view that the processes of governing now involve more diverse actors and more diverse organizational forms. Observers often speak, more particularly, of a shift from hierarchy to markets and networks.

All these new theories and practices of governance pose problems. They require people to rethink effective action, democratic values, and their relation to one another. As a result the word 'governance' has also been attached to various social and political agendas. Good governance is, for example, a mantra in current discussions of aid and development, although what counts as good governance is still a matter of contentious debate.

The theories, practices, and problems of governance come together in concrete activity. Theories inspire people to act in ways that give rise to new practices and new problems. Practices create problems and encourage attempts to comprehend them in theoretical terms. Problems require theoretical reflection and practical activity if they are to be adequately addressed.

Further, the theories, practices, and problems of governance all stand in contrast to older ideas of government as monolithic and formal. For a start, theories of governance typically open up the black-box of the state. They draw attention to the processes and interactions through which highly diverse social interests and actors produce the policies, practices, and effects of governing. In addition, the relationship of state and society changed significantly in the late twentieth century. New practices of governance find political actors increasingly constrained by mobilized and organized elements in society. States and international organizations increasingly share the activity of governing with social actors, including private firms, non-governmental organizations, and non-profit service providers. The new relationship between state and society admits of considerable variation, but it is an international phenomenon. The new practices of governance extend across the developed and developing world, and they are also prominent among strategies to regulate transnational activities and to govern the global commons. Finally, current public problems do not always fall neatly under the jurisdictions of a specific agency or even a particular nation state. Governance requires new governing strategies to span jurisdictions, link people across levels of government, and mobilize a variety of stakeholders.

A new governance

Governance can refer abstractly to all processes of governing. It supplements a focus on the formal institutions of government with recognition of more diverse activities that blur the boundary of state and society. It draws attention to the complex processes and interactions involved in governing. Governance can also refer, more concretely, to the rise of new processes of governing that are hybrid and multi-jurisdictional with plural stakeholders working together in networks. It describes recent changes in the world.

The recent popularity of the word 'governance' undoubtedly owes much to its fit with changes in the world. The state has become increasingly dependent on organizations in civil society and more constrained by international linkages. On the one hand, the public sector in many states has shifted away from bureaucratic hierarchy and toward markets and networks. Governance here echoes the ways in which patterns of rule operate in and through groups in the voluntary and private sectors. On the other hand, states are increasingly tangled up in transnational and international settings as a result of the internationalization of industrial and financial transactions, the rise of regional blocs, and growing concerns about global problems such as terrorism and the environment. Governance here captures the formal and informal ways in which states have attempted to respond to the changing global order. Issues of governance loom large in a world where government has become an increasingly complex matter dependent on diverse stakeholders with formal and informal links to one another.

Many of the ideas, activities, and designs of governance appear unconventional. An important feature of the new governance is that it combines established administrative arrangements with features of the market. Governance arrangements are often hybrid practices, combining administrative systems with market mechanisms and non-profit organizations. Novel forms of mixed public–private or entirely private forms of regulation are developing. For example, school reform often now combines older administrative arrangements (school districts, ministries of education) with quasi-market strategies that are meant to give parents greater choice (charter schools, voucher systems).

Another distinctive feature of governance is that it is multi-jurisdictional and often transnational. Current patterns of governance combine people and institutions across different policy sectors and different levels of government (local, regional, national, and international). Examples include various efforts to regulate food standards and safety. International food safety standards are commonly established in Rome by *Codex Alimentarius*—itself a joint body of the World Health Organization and the United Nations' Food and Agriculture Organization; but if the USA imports fish from China, the presumption is that Chinese officials at the national and local level enforce these standards. The practice of regulating food safety operates simultaneously at international, national, and local levels.

The third distinctive feature of governance is the increasing range and plurality of stakeholders. Interest groups of various sorts have long been present in the policy-making process. Nonetheless, a wider variety of non-governmental organizations are becoming active participants in governing. One reason for the increasing diversity of stakeholders is the explosion of advocacy groups during the last third of the twentieth century. Another reason is the increasing use of third party organizations to deliver state services. Arguably, yet another reason is the expansion of philanthropists and philanthropic organizations, both of which are becoming as prominent as they were in the nineteenth century. For example, the Gates Foundation has both mounted a multi-city effort to reform urban school districts and embarked on a massive public health campaign in developing countries. The increasing range and variety of stakeholders has led to the emergence and active promotion of new practices and institutional designs, including public–private partnerships and collaborative governance.

Yet another distinguishing feature of governance reflects and responds to the fact that governing is an increasingly hybrid, multi-jurisdictional, and plural phenomenon. Social scientists have called attention to the ways in which governing arrangements, different levels of governance, and multiple stakeholders are linked together in networks. Environmental scientists have shown how natural areas like watersheds or estuaries are often governed by networks of stakeholders and government agencies. Scholars of urban politics have called attention to the way urban, suburban, and exurban areas get organized in broader regional networks. International relations scholars have noted the increasing prominence of inter-ministerial networks as ways of governing the global commons. More recently, policy-makers, often influenced by theories from social science, have begun actively to foster networks in the belief that they provide a uniquely appropriate institutional design with which to grapple with the new governance. Joined-up governance and whole-of-government approaches are widespread in states such as Australia and Britain, in policy sectors such as security and welfare, and in transnational and international efforts to address problems such as those associated with disaster relief and failed states.

An aquaculture story

Despite the rise of the new governance, old ideas of government die hard. Many people still associate governing overwhelmingly with presidents, legislatures, and courts. Television, radio, and newspapers still focus on elected politicians and political parties as well as their debates and changing fortunes.

Because the new governance often appears unconventional, I want to illustrate it throughout this book with a series of cases. The first case is a story of aquaculture. This story exemplifies the new governance. It highlights the role of non-governmental actors, showing how governing can occur without the significant involvement of governments. The contrast with old ideas of government is stark.

Aquaculture is the farming of aquatic organisms such as fish. Salmon and carp are the two most widely farmed fish. Within the farms, salmon need feeding. Because salmon are carnivorous, fish food includes fishmeal—a powder or cake made from whole fish and the bones and offal of processed fish—as well as cereals and vegetable proteins. Our story concerns the governance of salmon feed ingredients in the European Union (EU).

The EU governs salmon feed mainly through its general rules on feeds. Many of these rules arose out of a broad review of food safety in the late 1990s. Harmful levels of dioxins appeared in poultry feeds in Belgium. The European Commission's Directorate General for Health and Consumer Policy became concerned that feeds were the weak link in food safety. In 2002 new rules defined feed ingredients as safe according to their impact on animal health, human health, and the environment. A new European Food Safety Authority began to advise the Directorate General for Health and Consumer Policy on technical, scientific, and management issues.

Since 2002 there have been few disputes about the safety of fish foods in the EU. However, in the mid-2000s environmental groups began arguing that aquaculture feed practices were unsustainable. The EU required feed ingredients to meet an environmental impact test, and they did so. But the EU's criteria referred only to the impact of feeds on the EU environment. They ignored the impact of harvesting raw materials of feeds when the harvesting took place outside of the EU. Further, most of the marine proteins used in feeds did indeed come from fisheries outside of the EU. They came from wild fisheries in Chile, Peru, and the north-east Atlantic. Some environmental groups argued that these wild fisheries were over-fished and thus liable to collapse. Others argued that although these wild fisheries were stable, they were being fished to their limit, so sustainable growth was not possible. Both arguments tied EU aquaculture to unsustainable international fisheries. Where aquaculture had seemed to solve over-fishing, it now seemed to contribute to over-fishing.

Debate raged among various stakeholders, including the environmental groups, feed companies, producers, retailers, and scientists. But although the European Commission recognized the importance of sustainability, it did not believe that it could govern beyond its territory. The European Commission did not think that the EU should regulate the imported fish feed, partly because it worried that the World Trade Organization might treat any such regulation as a technical barrier to trade against its rules. Nonetheless, the European Commission is currently trying to mitigate the situation indirectly. Instead of governing the import of fish feed, it is trying to facilitate the rise of replacement ingredients that are said to be sustainable. It is revising feed safety rules to include the use of animal by-products. Also, it has increased funding for research on feed innovation.

While the EU did relatively little to alter the governance of fish feeds, other actors introduced significant changes. In Britain, for example, networks of non-governmental actors created their own systems of governance. Here too environmental groups proved crucial. British fisheries typically monitored fish feed using the criteria of the Fishmeal Information Network Sustainability Dossier, which concentrated on the stock of fish. Environmental groups wanted the fisheries to use the broader criteria of the Marine Stewardship Council (MSC), which include the impact on bio-diversity and eco-systems. In 2005 Greenpeace led a campaign to make public the sources of the feed for seafood. It also ranked British supermarkets' seafood policies using the criteria developed by the MSC. Then in 2006 Greenpeace published a follow-up report on the action taken by the supermarkets. Some supermarkets, such as Iceland, had made minimal improvements. But others, including Sainsbury and Waitrose, had begun to make more dramatic changes, typically as a part of market strategies aimed at appealing to environmentally conscious consumers.

Sainsbury, Waitrose, and several other big British retailers, including Marks and Spencer, wanted to demonstrate that they had a robust sustainability policy in place. They set up various networks and partnerships among feed companies, producers, and environmental groups to agree on the meaning and criteria of sustainability for fish feed. There thus arose various private systems of regulation and governance. For example, some retailers introduced 'traffic light' systems that graded the sustainability of different fish stocks as green, amber, or red. They then purchased salmon only if it was fed by feeds that had a green (or perhaps amber) light. Fish farmers thus had to adopt green feed if they wanted to sell their products to the big supermarkets.

Big retailers are able to claim that they are being transparent about their purchase choices along the entire supply chain in a way that mimics the EU's rules about traceability 'from feed to farm to fork'. They have created a system of knowledge and codification that regulates aquaculture. As a result they govern fish farming and fish feed through their private commercial rules and market mechanisms.

These British market initiatives, in their turn, intersected with parallel activities by transnational networks of private, voluntary, and public actors. The World Wildlife Fund (WWF) began arguing that all feed fisheries should require MSC accreditation. It ran a series of Aquaculture Dialogues to develop global standards for responsible aquaculture. These dialogues then established an Aquaculture Stewardship Council to manage the resulting standards. By the end of 2010 draft standards existed for an Aquaculture Stewardship Certificate in salmon. The standards reflect negotiations and compromises among international stakeholders and among environmental, economic, and social goals. For example, although the WWF still views MSC accreditation as a long-term goal, it currently accepts alternative criteria of evaluation that place less emphasis on bio-diversity and eco-system impact.

Aquaculture governance thus remains a fluid and evolving set of practices that overlap but also conflict and that are constantly being renegotiated. Government is often absent. The key actors are instead voluntary sector environmental groups, private sector supermarkets and fish farmers, and transnational organizations such as the MSC and the WWF. Even when public sector actors are present, they are almost never legislative ones; they are usually officials from regional blocs such as the EU. These plural stakeholders cooperate in networks that operate across the jurisdictional boundaries associated with policy sectors and levels of government. They create hybrid arrangements that combine laws, regulations, and markets.

Governance and history

Governance is about processes of rule more than institutions of government. Further, under the new governance, these processes increasingly involve organizational hybrids that cross hierarchy, market, and network, and embrace multiple actors from the public, private, and voluntary sectors. Nonetheless, the reader should not think that governance is a recent invention. The word 'governance' has a long history. The medieval poet Geoffrey Chaucer wrote of 'the gouernance of hous and lond' [the governance of house and land]. Another way to introduce the coherence and the importance of the concept of governance is, therefore, to ask why it was prevalent then and now but not for much of the modern era.

The concept of governance has waxed and waned in opposition to belief in the sovereign state. When people believe in a unified sovereign state, they often talk about its government. When they do not believe in the state, they concentrate more on the complex and messy processes of governance. The word 'government' characteristically sits best with a moral or empirical belief in a homogeneous nation under a unified state. The word 'governance' evokes more plural moral and empirical visions.

A state is an organized political community under one government. It is a political institution that has a monopoly of the legitimate use of force within its territory. This idea of the state arose in the early modern era. The early theorists of the sovereign state did not describe it as something that already existed. On the contrary, they argued that people should make the state a reality or treat it as if it were a reality. They were making ethical and legal arguments in favour of the state. For example, Thomas Hobbes thought that having a single sovereign power over a territory would prevent civil war. International lawyers argued that formal recognition of the state's sovereignty would reduce conflict and lead to more harmonious international relations.

By the eighteenth century the modern state was being taken for granted. Instead of arguing for it, people were treating it as a fact about the world. This acceptance of the state reflected changes in theory and practice. In practice, many European states had become increasingly centralized and powerful. The previous century had witnessed a gradual consolidation of territories under single authorities. European monarchs had exerted their power over local lords, taken greater control of public finances, and created various administrative offices. Improved communications had increased the ability of monarchs to exercise military and informal controls over relatively distant localities. Smaller commercial republics also had become more centralized as a result of similar processes. Democrats accepted the idea of the state as a single sovereign power; they just argued that sovereignty resided in the people rather than an individual monarch. Finally, as modern states became more powerful, so they promoted national languages and symbols in attempts to foster social homogeneity.

Of course, even the most centralized and homogeneous societies included contests and conflicts among various groups. However, the growing acceptance of the sovereign state reflected changes in theory as well as practice. Nineteenth-century thinkers typically understood society and politics in terms of a progressive historical development. Many of them thought that human history developed inexorably towards civil societies and nation states. The state appeared to them as a kind of fulfilment. They believed that each society was based on linguistic, cultural, and commercial ties. They thought that the state was the sovereign power over one such society. They suggested that this sovereign power was embodied in government institutions that were separate from the society that these institutions both represented and ruled.

As the modern state became naturalized, so the word 'government' came to replace the medieval 'governance'. Although some thinkers always challenged the idea of the modern state as a reality or as an ideal, these thinkers remained a minority. Doubts about the idea of the state then gained considerable force in the early twentieth century as a result of two overlapping intellectual tendencies.

One challenge to the idea of the state was theoretical. The First World War more or less decisively shattered the belief in progressive histories. Also, discoveries in logic and statistics made new types of analysis possible. Social theorists rejected nineteenth-century narratives of the development of civil society and the state. They turned instead to more formal modernist

What is governance?

analyses. Indeed, it was only at the turn of the century that many of the social sciences arose as distinct disciplines separate from history and with their own professional associations and university departments. During the twentieth century social scientists increasingly discarded historical explanations and turned instead to formal classifications, correlations, and models. Many social scientists appealed to systems and structures and the location and function of units in these systems and structures. Other social scientists based their analyses on assumptions about the rational nature of individual actors.

A second related challenge to the idea of the state was more empirical. As social scientists rejected nineteenth-century histories of the state, they championed new topics. Some social scientists associated constitutional law and institutional history with the pre-democratic era. They argued that the rise of a mass society and the spread of the right to vote had created a new type of politics. They suggested that the study of this new politics should concentrate on political parties, organized interest groups, and public opinion as much as the institutions of central government. Over time social scientists thus began to pay more attention to political behaviour and the processes of policy-making.

Present-day uses of the word 'governance' arose out of these two challenges to the idea of the state. At first, however, many people thought that a hierarchic bureaucracy could insulate policy from politics. Bureaucracies had begun to arise in Europe as part of the process of promoting centralized authority and social homogeneity. Now, in the early twentieth century, people began to appeal to the administrative state as a counterweight to democratic corruption and populist excess. They argued that the bureaucracy could bring neutral scientific thinking to bear on policy-making. Government, conceived as the administrative state, remained apart from markets, networks, and society. Present-day uses of the word 'governance' thus arose initially in discussions of the organization not of public affairs but of corporate affairs. It was not until the 1970s and 1980s that the crisis of the state destroyed faith in hierarchic bureaucracy. Policy-makers then tried to reform the public sector by spreading market and network forms of organization. The result has been the rise of the new governance at the local, national, and global levels. As modernist theories changed the way people saw and made the world, so government changed into governance.

Chapter 2
Organizational governance

The resurgence of the word 'governance' arose from theoretical
and empirical challenges to the idea of the state as a unified
sovereign entity that encompassed people with a shared culture
and a common good. When social scientists challenged this
concept of the state, many of them adopted formal modernist
theories of social organization. Governance provided a theoretical
term to discuss general issues of social coordination irrespective of
whether or not government played an active role in such
coordination. Instead of historical narratives about societies and
states, social scientists adopted formal theories of organization.

Modernist organization theory characteristically provides typologies
describing and explaining different types of coordination. Most of
the typologies focus on three ideal types: hierarchy, market, and
network. Each of the ideal types relies on a particular form of
governance to coordinate actions. Hierarchies rely on authority and
centralized control. Markets rely on prices and dispersed
competition. Networks rely on trust across webs of associations.
Further, modernist social scientists link these different forms of
governance to other organizational characteristics, including the
basis of relations among members of the organization, the degree of
the members' dependence on each other, approaches to resolving
conflicts, and the general organizational culture. Box 1 provides an
overview of the resulting typology.

Box 1 A typology of organizational structure

	Hierarchies	Markets	Networks
Governance	Authority	Prices	Trust
Basis of relations among members	Employment	Contracts and property rights	Exchange of resources
Degree of dependence among members	Dependent	Independent	Interdependent
Means of conflict resolution and coordination	Rules and commands	Haggling	Diplomacy
Culture	Subordination	Competition	Reciprocity

This chapter will discuss abstract organization theories of hierarchy, market, and network. It is important to remember that these theories have influenced management and administration. Organization theories have led decision-makers to reform the governance of corporations, public bodies, and global affairs. Organization theories helped inspire the rise of new practices and agendas of governance.

Hierarchies

According to the *Oxford English Dictionary*, the word 'hierarchy' was first used in English in 1880 to refer to an order of angels. Before long, however, 'hierarchy' was being used to describe the organizational structures of public bureaucracies and private firms. Modernist organization theory arose out of the work of Max Weber (1864–1920), a German sociologist. Weber's study of bureaucracy suggested that it had a central authority based on rationality and law. This central authority presided over a chain of subordinate units that performed increasingly specialized functions. Each higher unit exercised command and control over the units immediately beneath it. Each lower unit was accountable to the unit immediately above it. During the early twentieth century, management theorists began to study the firm as an organization. Scholars wanted to understand the role of the firm in the economy, and also to help managers promote efficiency.

Hierarchies are thought to work best when an organization has a fairly clear purpose. Bureaucracies in the public sector are meant to pursue the public good. Firms in the private sector are meant to pursue profit. The existence of a clear purpose means that hierarchies can divide their activities into a clear set of functions that can be assigned to different units. Further, the function of each unit can be divided into sub-sets that can be assigned to sub-units. The result is a nested or pyramidal structure of units, each consisting of sub-units all the way to the bottom. There might be twenty units at the bottom, overseen at the next level up by seven units, overseen by three, which are then controlled by the one unit at the apex of the organization.

This pyramidal structure means that hierarchies can divide complex tasks into more manageable ones. Consequently, hierarchies encourage a division of labour and thus specialization. Each unit has its specialized function and specific tasks. Higher-level units coordinate the various functions of the lower-level units. Other characteristics of modern hierarchies follow from this specialization. For example, hierarchies often give great scope to written documents as guides and records of action, and they often recruit experts or provide expert training to take on certain tasks.

It is the pyramidal structure of hierarchies that makes management so important within them. Each unit has to manage the sub-units under its control. Decisions and rules often come from the top and flow downwards. Often the higher levels of the pyramid concentrate on devising and coordinating strategies and policies, the mid-levels then translate the strategies and policies into directives, and the lower levels put the directives into practice. Each unit needs to oversee and direct its subordinates in order to make sure that the strategies and policies are rightly understood and applied. Each unit commands those that are immediately below it. Each unit is controlled by that immediately above it. Strict rules and clear lines of authority facilitate oversight and accountability.

The members of a hierarchy are usually employees. They retain their individual freedom unlike, for example, slaves. But they have a contractual obligation to spend some time working on behalf of the hierarchy and fulfilling some task within it. Usually they are employed and later promoted on the basis of their formal qualifications, merits, and technical expertise. Wage levels and other compensation typically increase as people move up the hierarchy. Those further up the hierarchy often decide whom to promote to senior positions. Alternatively, issues of appointment and promotion can be handled by a particular unit within the organization. Throughout the hierarchy clear rules govern the behaviour of employees. When people break the rules, they are disciplined.

Generally hierarchies rely on a rule-based approach to authority. Hierarchy is an impersonal order. The places and duties of the people within hierarchies are defined formally. Although the relevant people may have personal relationships with one another, their professional relationships depend on their places in the organization. For example, when someone higher up the organization tells a subordinate to do something, the subordinate obeys less because of the personal qualities of the higher-up than because of the formal position of the higher-up as 'a boss'. Again, when subordinates have a grievance with a boss, they typically have recourse to a formal process of appeal in which their grievance is judged by reference to the written rules that govern the organization. Abstract rules and formal relationships thus define people's place in a hierarchy. Authority depends on the offices that people hold in the organization.

There is, however, some dispute about the nature of the authority in hierarchies. Weber argued that hierarchy went with a rational and legal form of authority. In his view authority can be charismatic, traditional, or rational-legal. Charismatic authority is always unstable as it relies on particular individuals. Traditional authority provides more stability by sanctifying historic customs, practices, and orders. In modern life legitimacy depends on a belief in the legality of a set of rules and in the right that these rules give people in certain positions to command others. For Weber, bureaucracies characteristically rely on this rational-legal authority to institutionalize abstract rules and relationships. In contrast, Herbert A. Simon later argued that hierarchies need not depend on any particular type of authority. He defined hierarchy solely by the nested structure of its units. In this view hierarchy need not be a top-down organization. Hierarchies can arise from subordinates passing authority upwards. Consent can be as important as abstract rules in sustaining a pyramidal structure.

Hierarchic organizations have some clear advantages. Their pyramidal structure allows complex tasks to be divided into more manageable chunks. It also allows routine tasks to be delegated downwards. More recently, organization theorists have discussed the advantages of hierarchies by asking why they arise. Economists predictably argue that hierarchies are a response to market failure. In this view hierarchies provide a way of reducing transaction costs and limiting exposure to risk. Alternatively sociologists argue that hierarchy corresponds to a modern western concept of rationality and that hierarchies spread along with this concept. In this view hierarchies provide at least the appearance of an impartial expertise.

In addition to being particularly efficient at certain tasks, hierarchic organizations have some widely recognized moral and political advantages. Liberal democracy is often thought to depend on clear lines of accountability: administrators must be accountable to elected politicians who are then accountable to voters. Hierarchy facilitates these lines of accountability by institutionalizing clearly defined responsibilities and relationships. Hierarchy makes it easy to recognize that a person P is accountable to another Q for the performance of a task T. Accountability is, moreover, an important aspect of many other public goals. The protection of human rights and the equal treatment of citizens depend on formal rules and relationships and on proper procedures of appeal. Formal rules and relationships are a barrier to corruption and official bias.

Although hierarchies have advantages, they also have limitations. Indeed, by the 1960s and 1970s many organization theorists had begun to emphasize the failings of hierarchy rather more than its advantages. Critics argue that hierarchies are unresponsive and inefficient. Hierarchies are unresponsive insofar as their employees concentrate on obeying the rules that apply within the hierarchy rather than on reacting to the wishes of those outside of it, such as customers or citizens. Similarly, hierarchies are inefficient insofar as their employees follow orders and procedures even when these are anything but optimal. Some critics point here to the effect that hierarchies can have on the minds of the employees within them. Employees might concentrate on their own safety or on improving their own position in the organization at the expense of the good of the organization as a whole. Again, they might appeal to the existing rules to protect themselves, not to improve their performance. In doing so they might become risk averse. The organization might then stagnate.

There are some types of task for which hierarchy seems particularly inappropriate. One example is tasks for which there are no clear criteria of success—perhaps including creative innovation. Hierarchies rely on the ability of bosses to supervise subordinates. If there are no clear guidelines on what subordinates should do or on how they should do it, then this supervision cannot work properly. It is difficult to deal properly with ambiguity and flexibility in hierarchical organizations that rely on formal rules and relationships. Another example is change and adaptation. Hierarchies rely on institutionalized roles and procedures. If an organization's environment changes, its established procedures may be of little use in the new circumstances. It can be difficult to adapt—and especially to adapt quickly and continuously—if one has to follow outdated guidelines.

Markets

As criticisms of hierarchy spread, so some organization theorists began to trumpet the virtues of markets. Neoliberals often suggested that markets and market mechanisms were some kind of panacea. The formalism of modernist economics typically postulated an abstract concept of the market as intrinsically producing an efficient equilibrium. By abstracting markets from history, economists could conclude that apart from a few exceptional circumstances there is no reason to replace markets with other forms of organization.

The idea of the market as a type of organization is an abstraction from an actual market place. As an abstract concept, however, a market need not have any particular physical location. The market is, in other words, a more or less formal arena in which goods are exchanged for other goods and especially money. So conceived, the market involves two parties voluntarily exchanging goods at a given price. On one side, there are sellers who have goods they bring to the market. The sellers create the supply of goods. On the other side, there are customers who want to acquire goods at the market. The customers create the demand for the goods. Interactions among the sellers and customers establish the price of the goods. The goods are exchanged for the market price. Generally formal analyses of the market suggest that the price mechanism means that markets tend to equilibrium. Markets are in equilibrium when the total supply of a good equals the total demand for that good. In theory, this equilibrium is the state of affairs in which none of the sellers or customers could make themselves better off by altering the amount of goods they buy at the existing prices.

Modernist economics includes two slightly different views of the market. The dominant neoclassical view emphasizes perfect competition. In this view separate firms try to maximize their profits by responding to changes in prices. Decision-makers have the necessary information about market conditions and prices. This information leads them to alter their behaviour by, for example, producing more of one good and less of another, increasing the price they charge for a good, or buying a new product. It is their shifting behaviour in response to changing prices that leads to market equilibrium. The alternative view of the neo-Austrian school emphasizes the competitive process. In this view the market is more dynamic. Neo-Austrian economists think of the market as a process of selection occurring in changing and tumultuous conditions. They suggest that the market is often in disequilibrium. For them, the advantages of the market stem from the impact of competition on behaviour and outcomes.

The market, especially in the neoclassical view, produces coordination through exchanges and prices. People who are widely dispersed and have no knowledge of one another are nonetheless reacting to one another's effect on prices. If people I have never met start to pay more and more for a good, its price goes up, and when I see this rising price, I receive information about their actions and desires. More generally, people start to produce more of a good when its price goes up and less of it as its price goes down. Again, people start to buy less of a good (perhaps substituting another for it) as its price goes up, and they start to buy more of a good (perhaps using it as a substitute for others) when its price goes down. Prices convey information to which people react by altering their actions. These new actions tend to restore market equilibrium. The desires of all the market actors are thus coordinated.

People's interactions in the market often reflect its decentralized nature. The market actors are largely independent of one another. Their interactions are impersonal transactions. These interactions occur for the purpose of exchanging goods. They can be isolated or episodic rather than enduring relationships. There is no need for market relationships to involve face-to-face meetings. Social bonds and levels of trust are thus relatively low in many markets. Instead, markets often rely on laws, governments, and the threat of sanctions to enforce contracts.

Clearly prices and competition are crucial to the market. In a pure market, prices provide all of the information that people need to decide how much of a good to produce and how much of it to use. This information effectively takes the place of the supervisor or boss in a hierarchy, for people order themselves in response to the information that prices provide. Competition ensures that if one actor fails to respond to prices while others do so, the actor who does not will thus suffer the consequences. For example, if other sellers reduce the prices they charge for a good, an actor who does not will have trouble finding buyers for that same good.

Because pricing information and competition are so important to markets, their absence generally leads to market failure. For example, competition can be undermined by monopolies and cartels. A monopoly exists when one actor controls the entire supply of a good. If a relatively small number of actors effectively control the supply, they form a cartel. Both monopolies and cartels enable those actors who control the supply of a good to keep the price of that good high. These inflated prices increase the profits of monopolists and cartel members at the expense of their customers thereby preventing the market from reaching a proper equilibrium.

24

The apparent advantages of markets are now so much part of folk wisdom that it might scarcely seem worth discussing them at length. The market's advantages are both practical and moral. One practical advantage is simply that markets can often provide a degree of coordination in the absence of a supervisor who has knowledge of desirable outcomes and of ways to reach those outcomes. Markets do away with the arguably implausible idea of a benevolent and perfectly informed planner. Another practical advantage of markets is that competition within them can force out the less efficient players. This competition can lead to the spread of desirable innovations. It can reduce the cost of the goods that people need or want.

In moral terms, markets provide considerable scope for individual choice. They allow people to make fine-grained decisions about how much more they desire one good in comparison with other goods. They allow people to modify these decisions from one exchange to the next. Provided people are able to pay the costs, they are free to choose from whatever goods or services are available. Some thinkers also argue that markets and trade involve social interactions and cultural exchanges that promote peace and security.

Although folk wisdom currently focuses on the advantages of markets, we should not let it blind us to the limitations of markets. Economists have long recognized that the use of a price mechanism involves costs that can outweigh the advantages. These costs include the time and effort spent getting relevant information, locating other buyers and sellers, discovering prices, and negotiating contracts. Markets often involve some uncertainty about transactions and outcomes, and it can be costly to reduce this uncertainty. Further, because markets can fail, they usually require regulation and supervision, which is yet another cost. Firms often keep tasks in-house rather than out-sourcing them precisely in order to avoid these costs. They might not want to have to negotiate for labour over and over. They might want to avoid uncertainty about the supply of their raw materials. They might want to have more direct oversight of an activity.

Because prices and competition are crucial to markets, the market is often an inappropriate type of organization if prices or competition are absent. Market exchanges rarely allow, for example, for their effects on third parties. Prices can thus fail properly to reflect both social goods, such as those associated with education, and social ills, such as environmental degradation. Likewise, monopolies and cartels can make it difficult to create effective competition. Prices can thus get artificially inflated for goods for which there are a limited number of suppliers, including natural monopolies.

Finally, of course, markets are often ill suited to the distribution of goods and services about which we have strong moral intuitions. There is no reason why we should assume that the outcome of market exchanges will accord with our collective sense of social justice. If they do not, we may have to decide whether the advantages of the market are sufficient to outweigh the resulting injustices.

Networks

For much of the first half of the twentieth century organization theorists focused largely on hierarchies and markets. Sometimes hierarchy and market appeared as the two ends of a spectrum. Other hybrid forms of organization fell somewhere between them. These hybrid organizations seemed less than ideal. However, towards the end of the twentieth century, a growing awareness of the limitations of hierarchies and markets led organization theorists to pay more attention to hybrids. The idea of a network arose as a third type of organizational structure.

Networks consist of multiple actors who are formally separate but depend on one another for key resources and so build long-term relationships to exchange resources. On the one hand, networks differ from hierarchies because they do not usually contain an authoritative centre to resolve disputes among the actors. On the other, they differ from markets in that the actors engage in repeated and enduring exchanges, often relying on trust and diplomacy rather than prices and bargaining. Examples of network relationships thus can include cooperative set-ups, coalitions, relational contracting, partnerships, and joint ventures.

Because networks consist of informal relationships, they presuppose a high level of trust among the actors. It is this trust that enables the actors to build and maintain their mutually beneficial links and exchanges. Yet, trust does not just appear out of nowhere. Rather, the actors in networks generally learn to trust one another precisely because they engage in repeated and beneficial interactions. As the actors experience being part of a network, they come to trust one another not to act opportunistically in ways that would damage the network. In a sense, therefore, networks get increasingly firmly established through a spiral of goodwill. Actors begin to cooperate for mutual advantage. As they do so, they forge closer relations and start to trust each other. This trust makes it easier for them to cooperate in later exchanges. The later exchanges build further trust and thereby solidify the network. Further, this spiral of goodwill often results in the participants in networks collaborating deliberately to try to strengthen their relations. When confronted with misunderstandings and setbacks, they attempt to overcome the problems in their relations rather than simply breaking ties with one another.

Social scientists have tried to create a typology of networks or at least to identify different types of network. Many of these typologies imply that the number and density of the relations within a network explain many of its other characteristics. Although the key characteristic of all networks is the interdependence of their members, the degree of their interdependence can vary. Networks are more participatory when the actors have roughly equal resources. These networks resemble self-governing associations. In contrast, if one actor has the bulk of the resources, that actor often plays a particularly prominent role in the network. These networks are often managed and governed largely by the lead actor. Yet another scenario arises when an independent actor, such as a regulatory agency, oversees the network. Regulatory governance depends here on an actor outside of the network.

Organization theorists generally agree that networks are more cooperative and egalitarian than markets and hierarchies. Networks replace the competitive relationships of markets with trust and collaboration; the actors cooperate voluntarily in pursuit of mutual benefits. Networks replace the chain of command that characterizes hierarchies with a flatter structure; whether the actors are individuals or organizations, they occupy more or less equivalent places in the network, each being dependent on the others.

A lot of claims have been made recently about the alleged benefits of networks. Some organization theorists argue that networks promote the reliable and efficient flow of information. In markets, actors often keep crucial information to themselves because they think that it might help their competitors. In networks, however, because actors trust one another, they freely share information. In hierarchies, information that exists at the top can be slow to make its way down to the lower levels where it is needed. In networks, however, there may be fewer rules and procedures blocking the spread of information to those who most need it. More particularly, networks often appeal as ways of crossing organizational and conceptual boundaries; networks enable different departments and agencies to come together to address a problem that transcends their individual remits.

Some organization theorists suggest that because networks facilitate the flow of information, they are particularly useful for mobilizing actors and promoting change. In this view networks make it easy for members to reach out and connect with other actors, forging loose ties that further extend the network. These connections can then lead all the actors to adapt to one another and learn from one another in what thus becomes a general transformation. Also, networks can give their members an independence from any central control and thus a freedom to experiment and innovate. The successful experiments and innovations then spread across the network as part of the general transformation. Some organization theorists argue, more generally, that networks are usually more flexible and adaptive than other types of organizations.

Even if networks have advantages, they are not without problems. One criticism is that they lack stability. Some scholars argue here that trust does not ensure that actors will not behave opportunistically and even undermine the network. When actors have significantly more to gain by breaking the norms and relationships of a network than maintaining them, they may be tempted to do so. Further, the informal nature of many networks means that if an actor behaves opportunistically, the other actors may have no effective recourse to either a hierarchic authority or a legal contract enforced through the courts.

Another criticism of networks runs directly counter to some of the claims made on their behalf. Some organization theorists argue that the complexity of networks makes them inflexible. In this view a change in a network depends on the consent of all the actors. As the actors are all interdependent, a single actor cannot change the network alone. Further, because each actor depends on the others, individual actors may find it difficult even to change themselves. A related criticism is that the complexity of networks undermines coordination and control. Many networks lack a centre capable of directing them. They can become fragmented.

Finally, criticisms of networks have a moral and political dimension. Networks blur lines of accountability. Their complexity and especially their lack of an overt centre providing coordination and control often makes it difficult to specify who is responsible to whom for what. Historically, administrative accountability has depended on clear lines of authority in hierarchies; each individual is accountable to their boss higher up the hierarchy. Networks typically lack such lines of authority. In networks, several different actors may come together to make decisions, act, and oversee the actions. Further, the different actors may not have a boss. They may be the collaborative members of a self-governing and self-regulating organization. Problems over the legitimacy of networks have a particular resonance in democracies, for networks can be relatively closed and a few vested interests can use a policy network to pursue their factional interests at the expense of the common good.

There is much irony here. Bureaucracy was popular for much of the twentieth century because it promised to control factionalism and vested interests. Bureaucracy was meant to provide policy coordination and to defend the common good. Since the 1980s, many organization theorists and policy-makers have turned away from bureaucratic hierarchies to champion markets and more recently networks. Yet, the spread of markets and networks has now led some theorists again to worry about factionalism and vested interests. The benefits of hierarchy are becoming clear again.

A story of academia

Although organization theory is abstract, it has had a dramatic impact on the world. By the late twentieth century decision-makers were following organization theory in promoting markets and networks. They tried to reorganize public bureaucracies and private corporations. They wanted to reform the hierarchies of the early twentieth century by introducing market mechanisms

Australian Government
Australian Public Service Commission

Tackling Wicked Problems

A Public Policy Perspective

Organizational governance

2. Social scientific theories, such as that of a wicked problem, have had
a dramatic impact on public policy in Australia and elsewhere

and network ties. I want to bring abstract organization theory down to earth, therefore, by telling the story of how one academic idea influenced public governance. The academic idea of a 'wicked problem' inspired a turn to 'whole-of-government' agendas.

When modern planning theory developed between the world wars, it promoted a rational approach based on centralized knowledge and hierarchic organization. Hierarchic institutions collected and studied data, evaluated courses of action, and implemented decisions. This rational planning was subject to numerous and spreading criticisms from the late 1960s onwards. From one side, neoliberals argued that rational planning was impossible and it created bureaucracies that were inherently inefficient and unresponsive. From the other side, progressives began to point to a lack of results and to the dominance of economic interests in the planning process.

The term 'wicked problem' arose in this context. Horst Rittel and Melvin M. Webber introduced the term in an academic paper first published in 1973. Rittel and Webber argued that wicked problems were particularly difficult to solve. They suggested that although rational planning had proved well suited to more 'tame' problems, it had been less successful in addressing complex and interconnected 'wicked' problems.

Most definitions of wicked problems refer to a list of features. Wicked problems are more or less unique. They lack definitive formulations. There are many explanations for them. There is no test to decide the value of any response to them. Each response has important consequences, so there is no real chance to learn by trial and error. Typically these features mean that wicked problems are interrelated. Any one wicked problem has complex links to others. Any response to one may impact others. Classic examples of wicked problems include pressing issues of governance such as security, environment, and urban blight.

Planning theorists argued that wicked problems explain the failings of hierarchies. In their view departmental silos undermine the coordination needed to solve intransigent and interrelated problems. Wicked problems require more collaborative and innovative approaches. People have to cooperate across established boundaries within and across organizations. Some planning theorists thus concluded that networks and partnerships could help solve wicked problems.

This belief in networks and partnerships encouraged decision-makers to adopt new programmes labelled 'whole-of-government' or 'joined-up governance'. In an official paper, *Tackling Wicked Problems*, the Australian Public Service argued that wicked problems challenge bureaucratic ways of working because they are peculiarly difficult to solve. Wicked problems require 'thinking that is capable of grasping the big picture'. They require 'more collaborative and innovative approaches'. And they require actors to operate 'across organizational boundaries' in a whole-of-government approach.

So, the Australian government adopted a 'whole-of-government' approach to wicked problems. Another official document explains: 'The distinguishing characteristic of whole of government work is that there is an emphasis on objectives shared across organizational boundaries, as opposed to working solely within an organization.' Land management provides an example. In 2002 the Australian government created a Natural Resource Management Team in order to promote sustainable agricultural production and environmental protection. This management team secures cooperation and coordination among various government programmes such as the Natural Heritage Trust and the National Action Plan for Salinity and Water Quality. Policy is formed by a multi-jurisdictional committee, the Natural Resource Management Ministerial Council, which consists of environmental and agricultural policy-makers from the federal level, the states, and local territories, and which is co-chaired by the heads of the Department of Environment and Heritage and the Department of Agriculture, Fisheries, and Forestry.

Academic ideas about wicked problems also inspired policy shifts at the global level. In 2005 the Organization for Economic Cooperation and Development (OECD) established Principles for Good Engagement in Fragile States. The Principles highlighted the importance of developing coherent programmes to span the administrative, economic, political, and security domains. The OECD created a new group to develop an explicitly 'whole-of-government' approach.

The OECD points to Canada's operations in Haiti as a good example of a whole-of-government approach. Canada relies on inter-organizational networks in Ottawa (the capital of Canada) and on the ground in Haiti. Canada's policies are devised and planned by an Interdepartmental Steering Group that brings together all the agencies involved. The steering group defines the broad procedures and budget for the operations in Haiti. An Interdepartmental Working Group then manages the operations. Operations on the ground in Haiti are primarily executed by the diplomatic corps and security personnel. The whole-of-government approach appears here in the emphasis on coordinating among these groups and between them and other actors. So, for example, the diplomatic corps collaborates with the international community and especially with Haitian officials, providing a channel for local ideas and inputs.

The cycle of modernism

Modernist organization theory concentrates on formal analyses of ideal types. As a result, hierarchies, markets, and networks often appear as abstract models with more or less intrinsic properties. There is a danger of organization theory bewitching people. For a start, scholars and decision-makers might forget that actual organizations are not abstract models. Actual organizations are made up of living people and their actions. It is people and their quirks, not abstract models, which determine the nature and behaviour of an organization. For example, a market consists of people acting for all kinds of reasons not all of which are in accord with the assumptions that neoclassical economists generally make about human rationality. In addition, real organizations do not correspond perfectly to any ideal type. The actions of the people in an organization generally muddle features associated with hierarchies, markets, and networks. For example, if a customer regularly buys coffee at a particular shop but forgets her purse one day, the shopkeeper might give her coffee trusting her to pay later, thereby bringing the trust associated with networks into a market relationship. Finally, although it might be reasonable to associate an ideal type with a set of properties, it is a mistake to think that these properties necessarily go together or that these properties necessarily appear in any organization resembling the ideal type.

Some organization theorists might intend their ideal types to be heuristic guides that help people think about real situations and make sensible decisions. There is always a danger, however, that other people will treat their ideal types as if they were infallible accounts of reality. This danger is particularly worrying given the impact of organization theory on the practice of management and administration. As organization theory moves from the academy to professional and policy worlds, so it often gets simplified. Even if social scientists think of their ideas as nuanced concepts, hypotheses, and simplifications of a complex reality, decision-makers often lose sight of the nuances and treat the same ideas as rigid and infallible guides. Busy decision-makers hear headlines and grab at solutions that present themselves as science. Tentative academic suggestions become dogmas. Cautious academic proposals become alleged panaceas.

As the ensuing chapters show how modernist theories have influenced the daily practice of management and administration, so they illustrate the danger of forgetting the human nature of social life and taking the idea of a social 'science' too seriously. Much of the history of the new governance consists of successive waves of modernist expertise. Each new scientific theory or ideal type appears on the scene as a panacea. Decision-makers try to solve various managerial and administrative problems by introducing a raft of reforms based on the theory. The reforms fail. Often the reforms have unexpected consequences that create more problems. Social scientists offer new theories to explain the failure of the reforms. Decision-makers turn to these other theories and introduce more reforms. So goes the cycle of modernist governance.

Chapter 3
Corporate governance

Much of the new governance arose because decision-makers introduced a series of reforms derived from modernist organizational theory. The impact of modernist theory on practice began with private firms. Organizational theories helped inspire new practices of corporate governance. By the early twentieth century some corporations had grown into massive enterprises. Small individual- and family-owned businesses continued to flourish. But corporations were often owned, especially in Britain and the USA, by a large number of dispersed shareholders. These shareholders had no real role in the day-to-day running of the corporation. The management of the corporation depended instead on a hierarchy of professional executives topped off by a board of directors. The board was meant to provide oversight and control of the lower tiers of management. As the twentieth century progressed, however, this hierarchic management was increasingly supplemented by attention to market mechanisms and network relations. Principal–agent theory helped to inspire new approaches to executive compensation with the aim of aligning the interests of managers with those of shareholders. Stakeholder theory similarly helped to inspire new approaches to corporate social responsibility with a focus on the maintenance of healthy and mutually beneficial relations between corporations and the diverse actors on which they depend. Corporate governance thus involves the interests of shareholders, the responsibility of the board of directors, the rights of other stakeholders, and appropriate ethical standards, notably of disclosure and transparency.

The modern corporation

A corporation is a private legal entity with rights and duties distinct from those of its members. The liability of the members can often be limited should the corporation fail. Nowadays people are familiar with huge private corporations, including Coca-Cola, McDonald's, and Toyota. However, the rise of the modern corporation was a twentieth-century phenomena.

In medieval Europe, churches and local governments were incorporated so that they persisted from one meeting to another. Chartered companies arose later initially to settle colonies and then to spread trade. Prominent examples included the Dutch East India Company and the British East India Company. Almost all of the early corporations were formed through charters issued by monarchs or legislatures. Indeed, the state did not only issue the charter that created the company; it also oversaw the activities of the company to ensure that the company acted in the public interest.

When industrialization spread during the nineteenth century, states began to loosen their hold over corporations. In 1844 the British Parliament passed the Joint Stock Companies Act, which allowed people to form private companies without a Royal Charter or Act of Parliament. In 1855 Parliament passed the Limited Liability Act, which insulated the directors of a company from full responsibility for the legal or financial failings of the company. Nonetheless, industrialization remained patchy and uneven, and it generally occurred within older patterns of organization. Throughout the nineteenth century most industrial activity continued to occur in small workshops. The owners of these workshops were usually master craftsmen who laboured alongside the journeymen and apprentices whom they employed. Even larger industrial enterprises, such as mills, were usually privately owned by individuals, families, or partnerships.

Recognition of the rise of the modern corporation came in 1932 when Adolph Berle and Gardiner Means published their classic study *The Modern Corporation and Private Property*. Berle and Means argued that in the modern corporation ownership is separate from control. Although their argument focused on the USA, much of it applies more generally. In the modern corporation ownership consists of transferable shares while control consists of managerial oversight. The shareholders who own the firm are often not the managers who control it.

The separation of ownership and control in corporations is neither inevitable nor universal. It is most pronounced in Anglo-American economies because something like it is built into corporate law in Britain and the USA. More generally, however, the separation of ownership and control reflects the dispersal of shareholdings in big corporations. The shareholders collectively own the corporation. But they often have relatively little interest in the day-to-day running of the corporation. They have their own lives to live and their own jobs to do. They often lack the time, resources, and power to have any significant effect on the day-to-day activities of the corporation. Consequently, control of the corporation rests with its management. The managers determine the day-to-day operations of the corporation. Much of the time they do so relatively free from shareholder scrutiny.

As shareholdings disperse, owners and managers generally come to adopt very different roles from those they occupy in smaller workshops, family businesses, and partnerships. Most shareholders do not work for let alone control the corporations that they collectively own. The financial benefits of ownership take the form of the interest and other payments made to the shareholders in exchange for their continuing capital investment.

Again, managers need not have any significant shareholding let alone a dominant one in the corporations for which they work. As managers, they earn wages for their labour rather than increased returns on any capital they have invested.

Principal–agent theory

Corporate governance concerns the rules and practices by which companies are administered, especially when the ownership and control of a company are separate. The separation of ownership and control creates a potential conflict of interests between the owners (or principals) and the managers (or agents). A huge amount has been written about this conflict, much of it under the label 'principal–agent theory'. Principal–agent theory is among the most important intellectual influences on the reforms associated with the new governance; its influence has spread from the corporate world to the public sector.

One way to introduce principal–agent theory is as an account of delegation. Throughout social life, principals delegate responsibilities and tasks to agents; the agent speaks and acts on behalf of the principal. Agency theory concerns the hazards and problems that can arise as a consequence of such delegation. Initially agency theory focused on the relations of owners and managers in corporations. Berle and Means initiated these discussions by pointing to the growing number of joint-stock companies. Here the shareholders delegate the management of the company to its managers, and moreover each individual shareholder has relatively little knowledge and power with which to govern the day-to-day activities of the managers.

Soon economists began to offer formal analyses of the agency problem. Their analyses of corporate governance explore the consequences of the self-interested nature of human action in contexts of asymmetric information. Typically economists assume, first, that individuals are rational actors pursuing their own preferences. So, although the shareholder employs the managers to pursue his or her interests, the managers will pursue their own interests. No doubt because the shareholder pays the managers, the managers will have to keep him or her content. Yet, economists assume, secondly, that the shareholder has only incomplete information about the intentions and actions of the managers. Because the shareholder cannot oversee everything the managers do, the managers can do enough to keep him or her happy while still retaining some leeway to pursue their own interests.

Economists argue that delegation gives rise to three main types of cost. First, the principal has to pay the costs of overseeing the agents. For example, the principal might hire an auditor to check on the actions of the agents. Second, the agent has to pay the costs of certifying to the principals that his or her actions are indeed in accord with their interests. For example, the agent might compile and present swathes of information to the principal. Finally, the principal has to bear any residual costs that result from the agents nonetheless pursuing their interests, not his or hers.

Responses to an agency problem try to reduce the total of these costs as far as possible. Economists usually identify two main strategies available to the principal. First, the principal can monitor the agents. The principal can devise a system for checking on the actions of the agents to make sure that these actions are appropriate to his or her interests. Second, the principal can make the agents share the consequences of their actions. The principal can devise incentive structures for the agents that make their interests correspond more closely to his or hers. The optimal response to an agency problem typically balances these two strategies so as to reduce agency costs as far as possible.

Many social scientists distinguish agency theory from wider discussions of the principal–agent problem. Agency theory appeared earlier and it concerns only corporate governance. The principal–agent problem extends the application of agency theory to other instances of delegation. In modern democracies, for example, citizens elect representatives to make political decisions on their behalf, and the elected representatives appoint bureaucrats to implement these decisions. Similarly, in modern societies, people hire lawyers, doctors, and child-care providers. All of these relationships can be seen under the right circumstances as involving delegation in a context of asymmetrical information. Thus, all of them can be modelled using agency theory.

In corporate governance the shareholders are the principals and the managers are the agents. Because the shareholders own the firm, the firm should be governed largely in accord with their interests and decisions, but the shareholders delegate the running of the firm to the managers. The shareholders, as principals, empower the managers, as agents, to act on their behalf. Yet, the shareholders cannot be sure that the managers actually will act in accord with their interests and decisions. On the contrary, the managers will have their own interests that they may pursue at the expense of those of the shareholders. For example, managers might use corporate earnings to fund a lavish business lifestyle, including company jets and hospitality suites, instead of paying greater dividends to the shareholders. Typically, moreover, the shareholders are unable constantly to monitor and oversee the actions of the managers. Consequently, the shareholders, as principals, need controls and mechanisms to ensure that the managers, acting as their agents, actually serve their interests.

Hierarchic oversight and control

A key principle of corporate governance is thus the rights of shareholders. The main issue of corporate governance is how to ensure that the rights of the shareholders are properly safeguarded. When this issue arose, corporations usually had

'Apparently many companies experience problems including: a lack of direction, poor accountability, lack of respect among members, pushing personal agendas, poor communication ...'

3. Corporate governance covers a multitude of sins

hierarchical structures. The top of the hierarchy was meant to control and oversee the lower tiers in order to make sure that the corporation did not neglect the interests of its shareholders. Corporate governance generally consisted of a centralized management overseen by a board of directors. The board of directors exercised hierarchic control over executives and middle-level managers.

The board's control and oversight of the Chief Executive Officer (CEO) remains an important aspect of corporate governance. The board is responsible for hiring the CEO. It vets candidates before hiring them, checking on their integrity and their fit with the company's profile. The board then works with the CEO to develop the company's strategy—although the responsibility for the execution of the strategy lies with the CEO. As the board helps to form a strategy, it raises issues and provides advice and access to resources. Generally, however, boards do not give directives to CEOs, partly because doing so might make it harder for them later to hold the CEO accountable. Decision-making and accountability are kept separate: CEOs make decisions, and boards of directors hold them accountable for these decisions. Equally, however, most corporations have rules that prevent the CEO from unilaterally making important decisions. Major decisions often require the prior approval of the board. Requiring CEOs to get prior approval for decisions is not just a check on their rushing ahead foolishly; it ensures the board remains informed and can take corrective action if needed. Throughout, the CEO is accountable to the board. Boards of directors can sanction CEOs, ask them to step down, and even fire them. The board provides oversight and control of the CEO. It is required to protect the rights and interests of shareholders.

Discussions of corporate governance still pay much attention to the structure, role, and responsibilities of the board of directors. Most boards contain a mixture of insiders and outsiders. Insiders are people who are employed or have been employed by the corporation or its subsidiaries. The CEO of a corporation, for example, is often a member of its board of directors. Outsiders are more independent of the corporation. The insiders provide specific insight into the relevant corporation. They have specialized information and experience of the corporation precisely because of their close links to it. The outsiders provide a more objective perspective and a more neutral oversight. They can prevent group-think and collusion among the insiders thereby protecting the interests of the shareholders. Indeed, most accounts of corporate governance emphasize the importance of the board having a majority of outsiders. Studies suggest that having a majority of outsiders on the board generally improves the performance of a corporation.

Insiders and outsiders characteristically contribute differently to the various roles of a board of directors. The insiders are especially important to the executive role of the board. They make crucial contributions to decisions about the administration, strategy, and future of the corporation. The outsiders are especially important to the monitoring role of the board. They ensure proper, impartial oversight of the corporation and its activities. Finally, some outsiders, and more rarely some insiders, also perform a more instrumental role. They provide the board with access to outside expertise and resources. For example, bankers and accountants can provide access to financial knowledge and networks.

Oversight and control continue from the CEO downwards. A balance of power is important here to the internal structure of a corporation. Different people or sub-divisions should provide a check on one another. One obvious division is that between the CEO and the treasurer. Another is that between the general operation of a company and its internal (and external) auditors. The auditors oversee the internal accounting system, providing an independent evaluation of the effectiveness of financial and other controls within the corporation. External auditors in particular should provide reliable financial accounts that enable the shareholders to oversee and evaluate the performance of the board and the CEO. Problems may arise if the auditors are not sufficiently independent of the corporation but rather also earning fees from, for example, providing the corporation with consultancy and other such services.

Some discussions of corporate governance suggest that the rise of institutional investors enhances the control and oversight of managers. As institutional investors are shareholders, their interests overlap with those of the other shareholders. Yet, the knowledge, power, and other resources of institutional investors make them far more capable of monitoring the day-to-day activities of a company than are smaller individual investors. The hope is, therefore, that institutional investors can help protect the rights of all the shareholders. However, there is no guarantee that the interests of institutional investors will align with those of other investors. On the contrary, because institutional investors have shares in a wide range of companies, their main interests can be in other companies or, more likely still, in the performance of the economy as a whole.

Market mechanisms and compensation

The rise of principal–agent theory increasingly cast doubt on the adequacy of a hierarchic approach to corporate governance. The board of directors, even if dominated by outsiders, does not necessarily privilege the rights and interests of shareholders. The members of the board might pursue their own agendas and interests at the expense of those of the corporation's owners. Before long, therefore, discussions of corporate governance began placing increasing emphasis on mechanisms that align the interests of the board and managers with those of the shareholders. The basic idea is that the right kind of financial incentives and other market tools are more effective than hierarchic controls in ensuring that agents act properly on behalf of their principals.

External mechanisms outside the corporation might serve to align the interests of managers with those of shareholders. Some economists argue, for example, that a well-functioning stock market creates an environment in which managers will concentrate on maximizing profit. The argument is that a fluid stock market means that corporations can be taken over by new owners. If the managers in a corporation fail to maximize profits, then other actors will see an opportunity to make money by taking over that corporation and reorganizing its management. The threat of a takeover encourages managers to focus on maximizing profits, and besides, if they do not do so, they will not survive. It is worth emphasizing that this argument about stock markets is theoretical. It does not suggest any practical solution to the principal–agent problem in corporate governance. It just implies that the problem does not actually arise provided there is a market in which to buy and sell shares. Further, there are contrary arguments that suggest decisions about takeovers are often based on criteria other than the extent to which the incumbent management is maximizing profits.

More practical responses to the principal–agent problem often rely primarily on executive compensation. Market-based approaches to corporate governance have led to widespread changes in the types of compensation paid to board members and senior executives. First, an increasing proportion of compensation takes the form of stock or options. Giving directors and executives stock means that they become shareholders so their interests move closer to those of the other shareholders. Second, both directors and executives are increasingly prevented from selling their stock during a fixed time period, or alternatively they face financial penalties if they sell before a certain time. Requiring or encouraging directors and executives to keep their stock obviously maintains their stake in the company. It also encourages them to focus on the long-term growth of the firm and its earnings. Third, an increasing proportion of compensation, whether as stock or not, depends not only on the performance of the individual but also the performance of the corporation as a whole. Linking people's compensation to the performance of the corporation is to link it directly to the interests of the owners. Finally, corporations have cut back or even eliminated many retirement programmes for directors and to a lesser extent senior executives. This change further increases the reliance of directors and executives on stock as their main form of compensation.

Similar mechanisms can bring the interests of all employees closer to those of shareholders. Insofar as employees are constantly present in a company, they are well situated to monitor at least some of its activities. But, of course, they too have personal interests, perhaps in working less or in more luxurious work conditions. Here too, therefore, there is a trend towards giving employees a stake in corporations as a means to align their interests with those of the shareholders. An example is the

Employee Stock Ownership Plans in the USA that arise because there are tax incentives for companies to buy their own stock and then allow employees to earn it through their labour.

The evidence for the success of these changing forms of compensation remains patchy. Some evidence suggests that when executives own shares in the corporation for which they work, their incentives and performance rise. However, other studies suggest that when CEOs own more than about a quarter of the shares, they become increasingly sheltered from outside pressures in a way that can adversely influence their performance. The most heated debates concern compensation in the form of stock options. The relevant compensation packages give executives the right to buy shares in the future at a more or less set price. Economists have noticed that executives can use options in ways that are clearly contrary to shareholders' interests. This danger becomes particularly acute when options are exercised in conjunction with share repurchases in which a corporation buys its own stock. The problem is that these share repurchases provide executives with a way to influence the value of shares and so of their options. Following a series of scandals in the mid-2000s, stock options have become a far less popular form of compensation.

Corporate social responsibility

Even if the managers working in a firm owe a particular duty to its owners, they may have other ethical responsibilities. By the 1970s discussions of corporate governance increasingly roamed beyond the principal–agent relationship between shareholders and managers. Issues of corporate governance clearly concern other actors. Corporations have an impact on diverse stakeholders—shareholders, managers, employees, customers, local populations, and so on. Further, corporations typically depend for their existence on an almost equally wide array of stakeholders—suppliers, creditors, customers, government, and natural resources. The general point is, of course, that companies are embedded in complex networks of natural and social relationships. Executive decisions and corporate actions have implications for all these actors, not just shareholders. Stakeholder theory suggests, therefore, that a corporation should seek not solely to maximize profits for its shareholders but also to respond to the concerns and interests of other actors. In this view corporate governance includes a more general social responsibility.

It is comparatively rare for the law to require corporations to engage in socially responsible activities. Corporate Social Responsibility (CSR) typically relies instead on non-binding agreements and understandings within networks. Corporations voluntarily consider environmental and social factors when making business decisions. The motives for CSR often combine moral and practical considerations. In moral terms CSR is about corporations contributing positively to the common good. In more practical terms CSR highlights the economic benefits to corporations of good relations with the network in which they are embedded. Corporations are more profitable, at least in the long run, if they maintain mutually beneficial relations based on trust with their suppliers, creditors, and customers, as well as with local communities and governments. The reputation of a corporation is one of its most important financial assets.

Approaches to CSR vary widely and are by no means incompatible with one another. One approach is community trade, often combined with community-based investment. Here corporations work with local communities to build infrastructure, capacity, and sustainable development. The Body Shop was an early exponent of CSR including community-based investment. It sourced local and sustainable products from marginalized communities, guaranteed a living wage to the workers in its suppliers, built long-term relations with the suppliers, and supported initiatives in the local communities of its suppliers to promote other projects of sustainable development. Box 2 contains the Body Shop's Fair Trade Guidelines.

Box 2 The Body Shop's fair trade guidelines

Community

We are looking to work with established community organizations which represent the interests of their people.

Community in Need

We target those groups who are disadvantaged in some way, those whose opportunities are limited.

Benefits

We want the primary producers and their wider community to benefit from the trade—socially as well as economically.

Commercial Viability

It has to make good commercial sense meaning that price, quality, capacity and availability are carefully considered.

Environmental Sustainability

The trade has to meet The Body Shop standards for environmental and animal protection.

Other approaches to CSR rely on imposing requirements and establishing norms among business partners. Corporations can decide only to procure raw materials and other goods from suppliers that meet certain ethical standards. The Body Shop was again an early exponent of this approach. At the end of 1990 it stopped buying ingredients that had been tested on animals. The Body Shop even played a campaigning role in trying to get others to adopt similar rules and practices. In 1996 it presented to the European Union a petition with over four million signatures against animal testing. Box 3 contains the Body Shop's ethical standards.

At times CSR seems to consist of little more than building philanthropy into a marketing strategy. Canon's 'Donate a Smile'

Box 3 The Body Shop's ethical trade standards

Employment is freely chosen

Freedom of association and the right to collective bargaining are respected

Working conditions are safe and hygienic

Child labour is not used

Living wages are paid

Working hours are not excessive

No discrimination is practised

Regular employment is provided

No harsh or inhumane treatment is allowed

campaign in Hong Kong was an explicit online CSR advertising strategy designed by the marketing agency Dentsu. The campaign literature said smiles were contagious, so when one person smiles they make everyone else smile. Consumers donated a smile by visiting Canon's Smiling Photo booth in Causeway Bay and taking a photo there. Each photo was cropped into the shape of a ten dollar coin, which could then be shared as an online emoticon in a way that was meant to increase the buzz around the campaign. Canon donated ten dollars to the World Wild Life Fund for each photo taken in the booth.

Perhaps the most common form of CSR is just for corporations to devise internal ethical codes governing the behaviour of their employees. Corporations provide training in ethics to their employees. They discipline unethical behaviour and sometimes reward ethical conduct. These systems of codes, training, and rewards all help to ensure that their employees comply with the relevant laws and norms and also limit their liability should their employees fail to do so. However, the impact of such hierarchic control and oversight is often limited. Studies of CSR highlight the importance of supplementing codes and training with wider efforts to establish an ethical culture within the whole organization. In particular, leaders and managers need to lead by example. When managers exemplify the standards of the firm and develop a reputation for ethical behaviour, those standards typically become the norm across the firm as a whole. Ethical conduct depends on informal networks.

The social and political context

Sometimes corporations engage in CSR for moral reasons or as a deliberate business strategy. More often, however, they are reacting to their stakeholders. They are responding to explicit or implicit pressure from employees, customers, and governments. Equally, of course, corporations can promote CSR practices in an attempt to put pressure on employees, stakeholders, and governments to modify their behaviour.

Social actors often play a particularly important role in promoting CSR. They can create expectations of ethical conduct. Social actors can even make their expectations formal and public. They can publish guidelines, recommendations, and rules that they expect corporations to follow. They can monitor and report on the extent to which the relevant corporations do indeed follow these guidelines and rules. Further, the rules can be used for various purposes by consumers, social movements, governments, and international organizations. Businesses and industry groups sometimes adopt the rules as a form of self-regulation. These kinds of guidelines and rules have spread along with the growth of social movements and concerns about CSR. Despite their growth, however, they are often ineffective; corporations ignore them. The impact of the recommendations and frameworks increases under certain conditions. The recommendations should address specific issues. Also, the relevant social actors should establish a process for monitoring corporations' performance in relation to the recommendations.

Governmental agencies have a range of policies by which to promote CSR. These policies can rely primarily on law, information, economics, partnerships, or a mixture of any of these. Laws require corporations to adopt responsible practices. The resulting legal frameworks can be enforced by the courts or overseen by a regulatory agency. Economic policies provide corporations with commercial incentives to adopt responsible practices. Examples include giving corporations tax breaks for introducing energy saving measures or for investing in deprived areas. Governments can also promote partnerships with or among corporations in an attempt to spread responsible practices. Informational policies focus on providing companies with knowledge that encourages and persuades them to adopt responsible practices. Typically governments use all of these policy tools to raise awareness of CSR, promote transparency, and foster socially responsible investment.

Stakeholder theory and CSR became increasingly popular in the late twentieth century. However, studies suggest that even when corporations adopt them, their impact can remain slight. Part of the problem is that CSR generally concerns voluntary ethical standards as much as legally enforceable ones. For example, the Sentencing Commission in the USA tried to establish a code of business ethics. This code remained voluntary, although if companies adopted it, they could avoid penalties should their employees misbehave in certain ways. The Commission soon concluded, however, that companies were often adopting the letter of the code but not its spirit. Companies were following the guidelines exactly as they were stated without making any significant attempt to solve the ethical issues that the guidelines were meant to address. The companies effectively subverted the code by, for example, appointing an ethics officer but then not giving that officer the authority necessary to have any impact.

A scandalous story

The ineffectiveness of ethical codes was one of many lessons people took from the Enron scandal. Enron was formed in 1985 as a merger of Houston Natural Gas and InterNorth. Enron's stock reached a high of $90 a share in 2000. But Enron's executives were using a series of accountancy loopholes, special purpose entities, and complex financial deals to keep debt off its balance sheet. Poor financial reporting and a general lack of transparency hid the debt from shareholders and other observers. The culture at the top of the firm provided ample space for bad habits and values. By November 2001 the value of Enron's stock had fallen to $1 per share. Shareholders had lost a total of over $10 billion. In December 2001 Enron filed for bankruptcy. It was at the time the largest corporate bankruptcy in America's history. Several Enron executives were later sent to prison.

Before the scandal Enron appeared to be an example of good corporate governance complete with appropriate controls, oversight, and compensation packages. Enron had a solid board of directors. The directors had shares in the company and most of them were outsiders. Enron's executives received compensation packages that included stock and stock options and that rewarded them directly for their performance. Enron's internal structure included an audit committee, taken from the board of directors, and an audit division, several of whose staff had previously worked for the Financial Accounting Standards Board. The company's financial reports received external validation from Arthur Andersen, one of the largest and most respected of the world's firms of chartered accountants.

With hindsight, however, Enron's systems of oversight and compensation appear flawed. Enron's performance-related pay schemes encouraged executives to focus on the high-volume deals and short-term profits that added most to their bonuses. Executives unduly neglected the quality of cash flow and earnings.

Likewise, Enron's use of stock and stock options as forms of executive compensation encouraged an excessive focus on share price. Managers issued statements and adopted dubious accounting procedures with the clear aim of creating and meeting expectations of growth and so inflating the value of the company's shares. The concern with stock market value became so important that the changing value of the company's shares was posted on its computers. In addition, because Enron's directors were rewarded partly in stock and stock options, they too had an interest in inflating the value of the company's shares. The audit committee only met infrequently and briefly. Later a committee of the US Senate suggested that members of the board had a conflict of interests that may adversely have influenced their oversight of the company's practices. It also became clear during the scandal that some members of the board and audit committee sold their shares before the company's problems became public knowledge. Likewise, Arthur Andersen, the external auditors, also appears to have had a conflict of interests. Andersen's Enron account earned not only $25 million in audit fees but also a further $27 million in consulting fees.

Although hindsight reveals flaws in Enron's corporate governance, some of these flaws reflected the norms of the time. For a start, the deregulation of financial services had led all the major accountancy firms, not just Andersen, to expand their services from auditing to consultancy. The theory may have required them to keep their auditing and consultancy services strictly separate, but the theory was often hard to enforce in practice. In addition, directors and executives were often rewarded with shares and share options. Many directors treated their position as a largely honorary one given to them in return for the good will that they brought to the company. The theory may have required them to use their access to privileged information in order to exercise vigilant oversight of the company on behalf of the shareholders, but practice often bore little relation to theory.

Enron's executives behaved unethically, and some broke the law. Nonetheless, the Enron affair was arguably a disaster waiting to happen following the 1980s and 1990s with their promotion of an entrepreneurial risk-taking ethos and their deregulation of financial services.

Other scandals followed Enron, including, in the USA alone, those that engulfed Adelphia, Tyco, and WorldCom. The plethora of scandals raised awareness of potential problems with deregulation. The scandals reignited discussions about the role of public governance in the corporate world. Many states introduced new regulatory laws or institutions. In 2002 the US Congress passed the Sarbanes–Oxley Act, tightening the laws governing accounting in public companies in ways intended to protect shareholders. The Sarbanes–Oxley Act created the Public Company Accounting Oversight Board as a new agency to regulate accounting companies. It also included measures designed to ensure the independence of auditors, strengthen corporate governance, and increase the financial transparency of corporations. A few people spoke out against the introduction of these new regulations. But the Act was passed in the House of Representatives by 423 votes in favour to 3 opposed with 8 abstentions, and in the Senate by 99 votes in favour with no opposition and just one abstention. Public governance had new champions.

Chapter 4
Public governance

As corporations exist in the broader social world, so they depend on forms of public governance to sustain and regulate them and the markets in which they operate. Most discussions of public governance focus on empirical arguments about the rise of the new governance. Indeed, the new governance, defined in contrast to older forms of government, is associated mainly with the public sector.

The progressives of the early twentieth century championed a faith in expertise and bureaucracy. Classic accounts of public administration argued for a clear separation between politics and administration. Many presented the bureaucracy as a stronghold of impartial knowledge and advice and so as a check on the factionalism, populism, and other excesses of party politics. People believed that the bureaucracy could initiate and guide intelligent action to solve social problems. The electoral process and politicians would dictate values and goals. The bureaucracy would then use its expertise to develop and implement policies to realize these ends. Bureaucracy represented an ideal hierarchic structure of administrative and professional expertise. Although there were some attempts to promote more 'scientific' approaches to management within the public sector, such as Planning Programming and Budgeting, these approaches were generally ways of increasing control and coordination within a hierarchy.

4. This cartoon from the *Daily Mirror*, 21 February 1919, shows how bureaucracies have long been lampooned for their 'red tape'

During the 1960s and 1970s a number of theories and practical problems began to erode this view of public bureaucracies. Public choice theorists argued that bureaucrats were not impartial experts and defenders of the common good but self-interested actors who were intent on advancing their careers and increasing the size of their fiefdoms. The expansion of the public sector fed worries of state overload; people worried that society might stagnate beneath the burden of supporting so many and such large bureaucracies. In the media and everyday life public bureaucracies were increasingly depicted as ineffective and unresponsive to the citizens they were meant to serve.

The crisis of faith in bureaucracy foreshadowed a rapid and widespread rise in markets and networks as instruments of public governance. Many governments actively promoted markets and later networks through a series of public sector reforms linked to public management, contracting-out, public–private partnerships, and joining-up. These reforms were what led to the shift from government to governance. They gave rise to the new governance, however that might best be depicted. Some social scientists argue here that these public sector reforms have created something akin to a differentiated polity characterized by a hollowed-out state, a core executive fumbling to pull rubber levers of control, and a massive proliferation of networks. Others argue that the central state still dominates policy-making and implementation although it does so through new policy instruments.

Public management

Public management is about making sure that the resources available are used as effectively as possible to realize state policy goals. It was only as belief in hierarchy declined and belief in markets swelled that public management got separated from public administration. As hierarchy fell out of favour, so did a view of public administration as based on external oversight and rule-bound organizations. Policy-makers adopted market-based reforms in an attempt to downsize government and to make what remained more efficient. These market-based reforms coalesced in the new public management and, in the USA, the reinventing government movement.

The new public management spread unevenly. It was most prominent in anglophone countries—Australia, Britain, New Zealand, and the USA. Even there, however, it did not follow any one pattern. In the USA many of the reforms arose gradually across different states and federal agencies. The reforms then accelerated under President Reagan and the reinventing government movement; the Reagan administration spread the use of contracting to devolve service delivery to third parties. In Britain the reforms were almost entirely a top-down affair, stemming from legislation and policy initiatives under the Thatcher governments. In both the USA and Britain the process of reform continued after the neoliberal governments of Ronald Reagan and Margaret Thatcher had ended. Elsewhere the introduction of the new public management has generally been more piecemeal and less ideologically driven. Indeed, there is some scholarly debate about the reasonableness of treating the new public management as a global movement as opposed to one limited to anglophone states.

Behind the new public management lay two different if complementary strands of thought. One strand concentrated on the introduction of market practices and disciplines into the public sector. In this view market competition creates powerful pressures for efficiency, innovation, and responsiveness to consumers, which are otherwise largely absent from public governance. The other strand emphasized the importance of giving public officials the freedom to manage. In this view state actors should concentrate on 'steering'—the formulation of policy—not 'rowing'—the implementation of policy and especially the provision of services. These two strands combined to inspire various reforms aimed at separating policy and delivery. Service delivery was to be contracted out to third parties in ways that would create competitive markets in the provision of those services.

Contracting-out usually privatizes the delivery of a service. One organization enters into a contract with another for the provision of a service. Different organizations thus purchase and deliver the service. Sometimes state agencies might purchase services from other state agencies. Generally, however, state agencies contract out the delivery of services to private or voluntary organizations. So, contracting-out involves public sector actors entering an agreement with private or voluntary sector actors. The agreement is usually a written one that is enforceable by law.

It is worth pointing out that there is nothing new about the state buying goods and services in the market place from other individuals and organizations. For much of modern history states have bought things such as offices, paper, weapons, and even mercenaries. However, contracting-out has definitely become more common since the late twentieth century. In particular many states now enter contracts with third parties such that the third parties provide citizens with services that in the mid-twentieth century were provided directly by the state. The third party delivers the services to the citizens, but the state still funds the services in that it pays the third party to provide them, and moreover the state is still usually held accountable for the outcomes. The state is the principal; the contractor is the agent.

State actors adopt various approaches to selecting contractors. The most usual is to call for proposals and bids. If the relevant service is common and straightforward, the state may treat quality as fairly assured and focus primarily on cost. In these cases bids are often sealed. The use of sealed bids helps avoid suspicions of favouritism as does the use of publicly announced criteria of selection. However, in other cases, quality may be much more important to the state, so the state may focus more on reputational factors and on building long-term stable relationships with contractors. In these cases the state may have more reason to replace sealed bids with negotiated contracts. Because negotiated and sole-source contracting make it difficult to avoid the appearance of favouritism, they are mainly used when there is only one plausible supplier—of a new technology, for example.

In addition to contracting-out, the new public management included market-related reforms focused on financial management and performance review. In the USA the Job Training Partnership Act of 1982 introduced a performance management system to the public sector. This system included mandatory performance measures, new rules and procedures for accounting, and the explicit monitoring and rewarding of agencies in terms of their performance. Later the 1993 Government Performance and Results Act required federal agencies to create performance goals, measures, and plans. Agencies have to provide evidence of their performance in meeting these goals in accord with the measures and by the plans, and they also have to provide annual reports of their performance to the public. In the UK the Financial Management Initiative, also of 1982, devolved responsibility for financial controls and altered procedures for accounting and reporting. Australia too introduced a Financial Management Improvement Programme at much the same time.

Today performance management systems are common in public governance worldwide. For a start, performance-related criteria play an important role in enabling the state to manage contracts. The state as principal can use stated goals, reporting systems, and rewards to monitor and steer the actions of the private and voluntary organizations that deliver services as its agents. Public managers can stipulate that the third party who is to deliver the relevant service should meet performance targets with respect to things such as price, quality, or customer satisfaction. In addition, performance management systems are also important within public sector organizations. Public sector managers can create contracts with those below them that specify the requirements and goals of their job and the rewards they will receive for meeting those goals. Relevant examples include performance-related pay for agency heads and other public officials, and also performance bonuses that are applied across a whole agency or organization.

Performance-based incentives are usually tied to bottom-line outcomes. They thus depend on suitable accounting and budgetary systems. It is no surprise, therefore, that public governance has moved dramatically towards budgeting for results. Much stress now falls on performance indicators, output targets, and evaluation. Many states have introduced some form of public service agreements explicitly linking budget decisions to planned targets and performance results. These agreements occur in the context of multi-year budgeting and spending reviews at higher levels. On the one hand, public officials are meant to be given the freedom to manage provided that they produce satisfactory outcomes. On the other, budgetary reforms are the means by which the centre attempts to exercise control in an increasingly complex system.

A prison story

Marketization was especially aggressive in Britain and the USA under the leadership respectively of Prime Minister Thatcher and President Reagan. Most of the contracted services had a kind of private sector analogue. Offices are cleaned and food is prepared in the private sector as well as the public sector. Similarly, there are often well-established private sector industries operating alongside public ones in education, health, and even energy. When the state contracted out these services, there were thus private companies ready to supply them. In some other cases, however, the contracted services had no private sector analogue; there was nothing resembling a market in such services. For the state to privatize them, new organizations had to appear. One example is that of prisons in the USA. The state alone has a legal authority to imprison people against their will. Incarceration is a power reserved to the state. The story of private prisons illustrates some of the sources, difficulties, and disappointments of marketization.

There was an earlier time when prisons sold either the labour of their inmates or the products of that labour. But these practices withered in the early twentieth century. Investigations revealed corruption among officials and abuse of inmates. Besides, even neoclassical economists had started to develop theories of public goods for which there was no proper market, and prisons appeared to be an exemplary instance of such a public good. Governments had to take responsibility for providing and allocating public goods including incarceration services.

When a new approach to privatizing prisons emerged in the USA, it was alongside the reinventing government movement. In the 1970s some state governments transferred funds for community corrections to local governments. The local governments used these funds on half-way houses designed to reintegrate prisoners into the community. Later in the early and mid-1980s local governments increasingly looked to private organizations to operate the half-way houses. Also in the early and mid-1980s the US Immigration and Naturalization Service began to explore the possibility of contracting out the detention of illegal aliens. By the 1990s the out-sourcing of at least some incarceration services had spread across many southern and western states including Arizona, Florida, Kentucky, New Mexico, and Texas. Private companies had arisen to manage federal, state, and local facilities and to build and manage new facilities for public sector actors.

The extent and depth of prison privatization in the USA should not be overstated. It is true that in the 1990s the capacity of privately managed prisons increased by about a third each year. But in the 2000s the rate of growth slowed dramatically to just over 3 per cent a year. Further, despite this growth, the industry remains small, covering only some 200 facilities—less than 5 per cent of the total throughout the USA. Finally, even when incarceration services are out-sourced, the role of private and voluntary sector organizations remains tightly circumscribed. The US courts have ruled that even when the state contracts out incarceration services, the state must retain control over the admission and release of prisoners as well as the legal custody of them; prisoners in private facilities retain all the rights of those in public facilities. Private and voluntary sector organizations take over the daily care of prisoners. The state retains responsibility for them.

What effects have followed the contracting-out of prisons? Ironically the answer seems to be very little. There is little sign of increased competition or innovation among private prisons. There have been some prominent scandals, but so have there been in publicly run facilities. Private prisons are very like public ones. Proponents of the new public management would be disappointed by the lack of efficiency gains, but equally its critics would find few signs of declining standards.

The private prison industry lacks real competition. On the one side, the market has few consumers. The demand for private prisons arises almost entirely from federal, state, and local governments and government agencies. In practice, moreover, relatively few of these contract for incarceration services. The federal government and just over half of the states have contracts with private prison companies, but the contracts cover only a small fraction of prison facilities. Besides, a vast majority of correctional facilities are at the local level, and very few city or county governments out-source them. From the other side, the industry is now dominated by a few large suppliers.

Private prisons have made few innovations. Several factors seem to have given rise to caution. It is thought that prisons in general require a hierarchic and ordered style of management. Many of the state actors who purchase incarceration services specifically require that their private providers replicate the policies and practices of public facilities. Because there is no private market for prisons, private prison companies recruit many of their prison officers from the public sector, and these recruits bring their existing values, norms, and practices with them.

The private prison industry has had its fair share of headline-making cases of corruption and abuse. The New York State Lobbying Commission fined the Correctional Services Corporation $300,000 for failing to report various treats and gifts that it gave to state legislators in an attempt to keep contracts. The Chief Executive Officer of US Corrections was sentenced to fifteen months in jail for paying nearly $200,000 in bribes to win and keep a contract to house prisoners in Jefferson County, Kentucky. Newspapers also reported the use of prisoners for unpaid labour including construction work at Lee County prison and renovation work on various churches.

Nonetheless, the evidence suggests that private and public prisons are generally more or less indistinguishable from one another. Private prisons generally provide quality of care compatible with that of public prisons. Prisoners are often poorly treated and their rights often violated throughout the USA irrespective of who runs the facility. One study found that the costs of prison services bore a closer relation to the size, age, and security level of the facility than to whether it was publicly or privately owned and operated.

The USA spends a lot of money on prisons and its prisons are overcrowded mainly because it has the highest rate of incarceration in the world. The obvious way to reduce costs and to improve conditions is not to privatize prisons but to make more use of non-custodial sentences.

Network governance

Despite the drama of the new public management, its impact was anything but clear-cut. New market-related processes certainly did not straightforwardly replace old bureaucratic ones. On the contrary, hierarchic bureaucracies are still the dominant form of public governance. Sometimes the market reforms were just never implemented; they remained policy proposals or stated aims that had little impact on practice. Sometimes the market reforms were implemented but the manner of their implementation created new bureaucratic institutions and new sets of rules. Sometimes the reforms introduced new processes but these processes did not replace the old ones so much as duplicate them; the result was two largely separate systems performing much the same functions. Sometimes the implementation of the reforms had unintended consequences—or just did not lead to the hoped for gains in efficiency—so the state later returned to hierarchic processes in an attempt to increase its control over the new set-up.

Marketization resulted, therefore, in an increasingly complex world. Generally market-related policy instruments did not supplant hierarchic ones; they supplemented them. Generally contracting-out did not produce anything remotely like a free market; it resulted in a proliferation of service providers and networks. Generally the central state does not ignore the activities of these networks and third-party actors; it tries to control and coordinate them—to regulate and steer them—as best it can.

When social scientists talk of the new governance, they are evoking the complex world that has arisen in the wake of marketization and the new public management. State power and state action is now dispersed among a vast array of spatially and functionally distinct networks consisting of all kinds of public, voluntary, and private organizations, all of which the centre interacts with in an attempt to secure its policy goals.

The proliferation of networks was partly an unintended consequence of public sector reforms. In addition, however, many states have actively promoted networks in an attempt to overcome the deficiencies of both old bureaucratic structures and new market-related processes. Policy-makers have introduced a second wave of reforms to promote coordination and strategic oversight and to combat both bureaucratic departmentalism and the unintended consequences of marketization and managerialism. This second wave of reforms concentrates on forming partnerships, managing networks, and joining up governance.

Although the creation of public–private partnerships (PPPs) is nothing new, it has become far more common. The big growth in PPPs dates from the late 1980s. Indeed, PPPs are to some extent an alternative to earlier forms of marketization and contracting. PPPs consist of one or more public sector actor combining with one or more private or voluntary sector actor. Because the idea of a partnership is vague, PPPs can vary from loose alliances to more formal agreements to coproduce a policy or service. It is helpful, however, to maintain a contrast with other forms of contracting by restricting the meaning of PPP to cases in which the parties agree to joint decision-making and production.

PPPs bring public sector and other actors together to coproduce policies and services. This emphasis on coproduction explains some of the other characteristics of PPPs. The actors in a PPP have an enduring relationship. They actively collaborate with one another rather than merely entering a contract. Each actor brings one or more key resource to the partnership including finance, property, authority, and legitimacy. The actors share at least some of the responsibilities and risks that go with the project. Because PPPs involve closer relations among actors than do contracts, PPPs typically rely on a high level of trust.

Although PPPs can arise for all kinds of reasons, one paradigmatic case is when the state provides a private sector actor with guarantees and legitimacy in return for the private sector actor funding a public project. For example, a private corporation might build a highway in return for the state guaranteeing it a certain income to arise from tolls charged to cars that use the highway once it is built. Another paradigmatic case is when the central state provides funds and other support to local governments and community organizations to help them provide public goods. For example, the central state might support a local authority, a housing cooperative, and a coalition of local businesses engaged in a redevelopment programme including low-rent homes.

PPPs are in many ways just more formal versions of the networks that dominate so much of public governance today. Networks can be deliberately created partnerships, but they can also be more informal alliances between, for example, community-based groups, local shops, and schools, and they can span multiple geographic levels to include local, regional, national, transnational, and international actors. The rise of partnerships and networks more generally places a premium on the ability of public managers to steer them.

Network management is about influencing the organizations in that network. The aim of the manager is to promote their own goals and hopefully the goals of the network as a whole. It is important to remember, however, that all the members of a network often try to steer that network, so network management gets diffused and negotiated across the whole network. One of the main characteristics of network governance is, therefore, the relative absence of a single centre controlling activities. Each organization—including the relevant public agencies—has to negotiate with others. Even when a state agency has a formal and legitimate role to play in overseeing and coordinating a network, there will still be other actors within the network who are also trying to manage it.

Most of the leading tasks of network managers reflect the fact that networks contain interdependent actors. Managers have to promote trust among these actors. They have to manage conflicts among the actors. They have to maintain commitment among the actors. They have to try to keep decision-making processes focused on the shared goals of network members. Sometimes they have to manage the network's interactions with the wider social environment, perhaps recruiting new members to the network.

Finally, as the proliferation of networks has fragmented public governance, so policy-makers have looked to whole-of-government agendas and joined-up governance. As marketization has multiplied the number of organizations involved in governance, so whole-of-government agendas attempt to span multiple organizations and thus increase the coordination, effectiveness, and efficiency of public governance. Many intractable problems, including inner-city crime, social exclusion, and post-conflict reconstruction, are beyond the scope of any one government agency. These wicked problems require cooperation among a range of different organizations—central and local state actors as well as voluntary and private ones. Whole-of-government approaches try to promote an integrated approach to policy development and service delivery. The new governance is a complex world of multiple sectors and levels of policy each of which contains networks of public, private, and voluntary organizations.

A mental health story

Network governance is a much discussed topic. Some social scientists view it as a solution to all kinds of problems. Others worry about its impact on democracy. Yet others question the extent to which it exists. Yet, studies of network governance almost always focus on official policies. They rarely provide any sense of how citizens experience the networks in their daily lives. The following story does. It comes from the files of social workers employed by a local authority in the north of England. This story illustrates the impact of a multi-agency approach to social services on the life of one woman and her family. It suggests that citizens can be confused and overwhelmed by the complexity and lack of oversight in much network governance.

Mrs K was admitted to the local psychiatric hospital having become aggressive towards her daughter. Mrs K was 78 years old and had been suffering from dementia for two years. She lived

Governance

alone in a large detached Victorian house in a village some 10 miles from the local town.

Before admission, Mrs K's family, particularly her daughter and two children, visited daily and Mrs K had been coping well. The GP and Consultant Psycho-Geriatrician kept in regular contact with the family and a community psychiatric nurse visited once a week. Mrs K attended the specialist day hospital one day a week and the local elderly persons' day care centre one day a week. The social services Home Help service called in the morning (Monday to Friday) to see that Mrs K was dressed, breakfasted, and ready for any transport that would be calling. On the days Mrs K was at home the home help called at lunchtime to make sure that she had eaten the hot meal delivered by Women's Royal Voluntary Service or the home help (prepared at the local elderly persons' home). The family called in at teatime and again later in the evening to check Mrs K was all right. Mrs K tended not to sleep at night and would telephone neighbours in the middle of the night for help. She had been known to wander out in the middle of the night disturbing the neighbours.

To give the family a break Mrs K was admitted to the local elderly persons' home for a two-week short stay. After two days Mrs K became confused and disoriented, demanding to go home. The home manager became concerned when Mrs K began to wander outdoors, something she had not done while attending day care. Mrs K hit a member of staff who had tried to escort her indoors. A decision was made to allow Mrs K to go to the day hospital as usual and arrangements were made for her to return home.

On returning home Mrs K became even more disoriented, wanting to return to her home to be with 'mummy and daddy'. She hit her daughter when her daughter tried to take her around the house to convince her that she was at home. The daughter broke down, saying that the family could no longer cope and that she could not allow her children to visit if Mrs K was going to be violent.

The Consultant visited and decided that Mrs K needed reassessment and a review of her medication. She was admitted to the psychiatric hospital. The assessment showed that Mrs K's condition had deteriorated rapidly into a delusional and challenging phase. No long-term beds were available from the health trust but, with the correct medication, Mrs K's condition and behaviour could be reasonably well controlled. Mrs K was referred for permanent care to the social services care manager attached to the hospital.

The care manager decided that Mrs K needed 24-hour supervision and assistance with all aspects of daily living and personal care. The care manager discussed this with the family who were clearly distressed at the idea of nursing home care for Mrs K. With the new medication, Mrs K was less aggressive and they believed that they could manage with a full package of care for Mrs K. They insisted that Mrs K returned home.

The Care Plan was complicated and expensive. Cover for each hour of 24 hours was worked out for two-week blocks. The Care Plan involved the health trust's psychiatric day services, private nursing home day care, private agency home care, voluntary home care sitting services, social services home care, and several transport services supporting the daughter to provide 24-hour care at home. The social services felt that it would be more cost-effective for Mrs K to go into a nursing home. Following recent case law the local authority was within its rights to offer nursing home care to meet the need. They could have asked the family to supplement the cost of the care.

Because there were continuing health care issues, the care manager was able to secure funding from the joint-finance continuing care fund for the first four weeks. The care manager was unhappy about the arrangements because it is widely known, and particularly in the case of Mrs K, that constant changes in carers and location add to disorientation and confusion for people with dementia.

The daughter was concerned that she would have to give up work and asked if a private agency could be bought in for the equivalent amount of money. This would not help. There would continue to be many carers visiting. The house would seem like 'a railway station' with so many people calling.

The arrangements were set up on discharge but quickly become difficult to manage as Mrs K would not attend day care some days and more care had to be bought in from the private home care agency. There were frequent problems with maintaining regular home care support with home carers being ill, late, or not turning up and replacements being difficult to find in a rural area. Mrs K's son and daughter-in-law did what they could to help but they did not live locally and were not as committed as was their sister.

After one month the care manager decided to approach Community Service Volunteers, a national volunteer agency that provides young volunteers as full-time live-in carers. Four weeks later two young volunteers began providing 24-hour care and supervision for Mrs K. The care plan covered a three-week block with supplementary help for the community service volunteers. The cost of the care was similar. Two months later the young volunteers were feeling the stresses and strains of caring full-time for an elderly person with dementia. They were fighting among themselves and one young person began taking the medication prescribed for Mrs K and drinking alcohol. She was asked to leave.

One week later Mrs K died.

Rethinking the state

There is no doubt that local and central governments alike have been transformed by successive waves of public sector reform. However, there remains some debate about the consequences of these reforms. The heart of the debate concerns the current nature of the state.

Some social scientists argue that the new public management and network governance have hollowed out the state. They believe that fragmentation confounds centralization. In this view the state was already characterized by baronies and policy networks. The state was only intermittently and selectively able to control and coordinate policies and services. Now, the argument continues, the state has been further hollowed out by the unintended consequences of marketization, which fragmented service delivery, multiplied networks, and diversified the membership of networks. A segmented executive may have tried to improve horizontal coordination among departments and agencies and vertical coordination between departments and their networks of organizations, but the unintended consequence was still a weaker state. The new governance has undermined the ability of the state to act effectively. The state has become increasingly reliant on other actors and on diplomacy. Today, therefore, central control and coordination are modest at best. Even at the centre, there is persistent compartmentalization. Relations among powerful bureaux and ministries are characterized by mutual avoidance and unsuccessful attempts at reducing friction. Even when coordination is cooperative, anchored at the lower levels of the state machine, and organized by specific established networks, it still depends on a culture of dialogue in vertical relations and by horizontal integration. Coordination is rarely strategic. Attempts to create proactive strategic capacity for long-term planning are rarely successful.

Accounts of a hollow state are evocative, but they are at best partially correct. For a start, claims about the hollow state need to be made geographically specific. Generally they rely on an implicit contrast with a stronger central state implementing policy and providing services. Although this idea of a strong state captures aspects of post-war Europe, it is far less applicable to many other parts of the world. Large parts of the developing world have long had relatively weak states that lack the capacity to exercise any meaningful control. Similar problems also affected local and urban governance in the USA and Europe. In all these contexts the new governance is better characterized not as a hollowing out of the state but as an attempt to overcome the weakness of the state. The new governance can increase the capacity of public sector actors by providing them with policy instruments that enable them to operate more effectively particularly in contexts that are characterized by diffuse power, conflicts, and overlapping dependencies.

Even when the state has been hollowed out, there has also been a shift in the policy instruments on which the state relies. Metagovernance is the umbrella concept that best describes the role of the state and its characteristic policy instruments under the new governance. As governing has become distributed among various private, voluntary, and public actors, so the role of the state has shifted from the direct governance of society to the more indirect governance of the several modes of intervention. Again, as power and authority have become more decentralized and fragmented among networks, so the state has come to rely less on command and control through bureaucracy and more on indirect steering of relatively autonomous stakeholders.

Metagovernance refers to the new role of the state in securing coordination in governance. It suggests that the state relies increasingly on negotiation, diplomacy, and informal modes of steering. The state increasingly steers and regulates sets of complex organizations, governments, and networks, rather than rowing by directly providing services through its own bureaucracies. Other organizations undertake much of the work of governing. They implement policies and they provide public services. Sometimes they even regulate themselves. Further, these other organizations characteristically have a degree of autonomy from the state. They are often voluntary or private sector groups or they are governmental agencies or tiers of government separate from the core executive. The role of the central state is now to govern these other organizations as they govern civil society. The state governs their governance.

The state cannot govern other organizations solely by the instruments that work in bureaucracies. Under metagovernance, the state relies on alternative instruments to steer the other actors involved in governance. For a start, the state sets rules for other actors and then leaves them to do what they will within those rules. Here the state can redesign markets, reregulate policy sectors, and introduce constitutional change. In addition, the state can try to steer other actors using storytelling. It can organize dialogues, and foster meanings, beliefs, and identities among the relevant actors. Also, the state can steer by its distribution of resources including money and authority. It can play a boundary spanning role, alter the balance between actors in a network, act as a court of appeal when conflict arises, rebalance the mix of governing structures, and step in when network governance fails. Of course, the state need not adopt a single uniform approach to metagovernance. It can use different approaches in different settings and at different times.

Some social scientists argue that the new governance has increased the control of the state over society. In this view states have expanded the mix of policy instruments. As the older coercive and regulatory instruments became less important, states developed softer instruments by which to realize their intentions and control other actors. In this view the state has emphatically not been hollowed out. Rather, the state has reasserted its capacity to govern by regulating the mix of governing structures such as markets and networks and by deploying indirect instruments of control.

There may be some disagreements between those who see a hollowing out of the state and those who see the emergence of a powerful new metagovernance. Nonetheless, they also agree that there has been a shift from hierarchy to markets and networks, that this shift means the state has adopted a less hands-on role, and that the central state is less active in the provision of services and more active in the quangos that steer, coordinate, and regulate the other actors who provide services.

The variety of governance

The problem with most debates about the new governance is that because they rely on modernist assumptions, they obscure the variety and contingency of governance. Social scientists characteristically look for formal accounts of the new governance. They often define the new governance, for example, in terms of multiplying networks replacing old-style bureaucratic hierarchies. These formal accounts latch on to one or more defining features, and they then suggest that this defining feature explains other pertinent features of the new governance. The spread of networks allegedly explains the greater reliance of states on 'trust' and 'diplomatic' styles of management. Likewise, the spread of networks allegedly explains the search for coordination through joint ventures, partnerships, and holistic governance.

Again, social scientists often explain the emergence of the new governance by appealing to inexorable and impersonal forces such as the functional differentiation of the state or the marketization of the public sector. One common explanation begins with policy networks or sets of organizations clustered around a major government function or department. These organizations might include the professions, trade unions, and big business. Government departments allegedly need the cooperation of these organizations to implement policies and deliver services. More generally, the government has to aggregate interests if it is to set workable limits to the number of organizations it has to consult. The organizations in turn need the money and authority that only government can provide. The explanation of the new governance then turns to the impact of public sector reforms on these policy networks. Governments tried to bypass existing policy networks by using marketization and rigorous financial and management controls. But the reforms had unintended consequences. They fragmented the systems for delivering public services and they created pressures for organizations to cooperate with one another in delivering services. Marketization multiplied the networks it aimed to replace. Fragmentation created new networks. It also increased membership in existing networks by incorporating the private and voluntary sectors. Governments swapped direct for indirect controls.

Modernist accounts and explanations of the new governance imply that we can define it by reference to one or more of its essential properties. They imply that these properties are general ones that characterize all cases of the new governance: we find governance in its contemporary guise if and only if we find a spread of networks. They imply, finally, that these essential properties can explain at least the most significant other features of contemporary governance. Arguably, however, it is only modernist social science that makes these implications seem at all plausible. Surely practices of governance are products of people's actions. Surely people's actions are not determined by institutional norms or some logic of modernization but rather reflect their agency and intentionality. Surely governance is constructed differently by numerous actors grappling with different issues in different contexts against the background of different traditions.

A better grasp of the new governance might arise from accepting that it does not have any essential properties. 'The new governance' is a loose phrase that describes a number of overlapping changes, none of which need always be present. It refers to the uneven and contested growth of processes of governing associated with market and network organizations and mechanisms.

The new governance is not monolithic. On the contrary, part of the point of the term 'governance' should be to provide a more diverse view of state authority and its exercise. The notion of the central state being in control of itself and civil society is a myth. The myth obscures the reality of diverse state practices that escape the control of the centre because they arise from the contingent actions of diverse actors at the boundary of state and civil society.

The state is not monolithic and it negotiates with others. Policy arises from interactions in networks of organizations. Patterns of rule cross the public, private, and voluntary sectors. The boundaries between state and civil society are blurred. Transnational and international links and flows always disrupt national borders. In short, state authority is constantly being remade, negotiated, and contested in widely different ways in widely varying everyday practices.

From this perspective, state actors struggle—perhaps successfully but often not—to govern and steer other actors. Analyses of metagovernance reveal the various policy instruments and ruling practices by which state actors pursue control and coordination. Equally, accounts of the hollowing out of the state reveal the various ways in which state actors are thwarted in their pursuit of control and coordination. State actors meet others that challenge, ignore, or simply misunderstand them. Below them they meet voluntary and private sector actors in markets and networks. Level with them they confront other state departments and agencies. Above them they find transnational and international organizations.

Instead of looking for comprehensive accounts and explanations of the new governance, we might accept that the nature of metagovernance and the limitations of state action vary widely from case to case. The new governance is a complex policy environment in which an increasing number of actors are forging various practices by deploying a growing range of strategies and instruments across multiple jurisdictions, territories, and levels of government.

Chapter 5
Global governance

Debates about the changing nature of the state are inseparable from those about global governance. States exist in a world order, and dramatic changes in the world order rarely leave states unaffected. Many social scientists believe that globalization has been a driving force behind the hollowing out of the state and the rise of metagovernance. The ability of the state to govern within its borders has been eroded or at least altered by the rise of regional blocs such as the European Union (EU), the growth of global exchanges, and the increased mobility of finance capital.

Above the state, there are international relations. Yet 'global governance' now challenges 'international relations' as the preferred moniker for politics above the state. Here the term 'global governance', like 'governance' generally, has a broad theoretical and a narrower empirical meaning. In theoretical debates global governance offers a new way of thinking about international relations. Social scientists have long conceived of international relations almost exclusively in terms of sovereign states. The weakness of international institutions suggested that the society of states was an anarchic one lacking government. Sovereign states constructed the world order largely by pursuing their own interests in the absence of an effective system of international law and world government. The theoretical contribution of the term 'global governance' is that it, in contrast, implies that all kinds of actors might contribute to transnational and international orders, establishing forms of governance even in the absence of an effective world government.

In more empirical debates global governance refers to an apparent change in the nature of international relations. As globalization has contributed to the change in public governance, so it has led to a shift in global governance. The nineteenth century was dominated by empires and the balance of power. The two world wars inspired attempts to build a more stable world based initially on the League of Nations and later on the United Nations (UN). These international institutions were largely unsuccessful efforts to mimic hierarchic approaches to public governance. They were even accompanied by attempts to craft functionally defined organizations and to spread rational planning. By the end of the twentieth century, however, globalization seemed to have created, and also to require, a new approach based less on formal institutions and hierarchy than civil society, markets, and networks.

Theories of international relations

At a general level global governance offers a new theoretical lens through which to view international relations. This lens highlights the role of diverse social actors as well as states in securing patterns of rule at the transnational and global levels. It allows that patterns of rule can arise without hierarchic institutions let alone an international sovereign power. The lens of global governance thus stands in contrast to older theories of international relations that privileged states and formal institutions such as the UN.

The main older theories of international relations are realism and liberalism. Realists conceive of international relations in terms of sovereign states pursuing their interests in an anarchic system. In this view each state is an isolated and monolithic entity. The foreign policy of a state is independent of its domestic policy. Each state pursues security and power as they are given to it by the wider international system. Whereas domestic politics is orderly and conducted within a constitutional framework, international politics is all about power and anarchy. Realists associate their theory with Thucydides' history of the power-politics between Athens and Sparta and with Thomas Hobbes's picture of the state of nature.

Liberals accept much of the realist picture while insisting it is not immutable. Liberal philosophers, such as Immanuel Kant, and liberal politicians, such as Woodrow Wilson, emphasized the possibility of perpetual peace. Initially they looked optimistically to the beneficial effects of the spread of trade and civilization. By the twentieth century, however, most liberals rested their hopes on a dramatic strengthening of international law and international institutions.

Both realists and liberals present international relations as an anarchical system in which states interact by trade, war, and diplomacy. They suggest that the defining feature of international relations is the absence of any effective world government controlling, regulating, and coordinating the actions of states. Realists largely accept this picture and seek to work within it. Liberals hope to transform it by bolstering international law and international institutions.

In contrast to both realism and liberalism, the term 'governance' highlights the possibility that governing can occur without an effective sovereign power. Control can arise when actors internalize informal norms as well as when an external power imposes rules. Regulation can occur when actors monitor themselves as well as when an external power supervises them. Coordination can be the result of mutual adjustments among actors as well as of rules in a hierarchic organization.

The term 'global governance' draws attention, therefore, to the diverse activities and processes that organize international relations. Global governance is often defined in terms of any activity that contributes to transnational and international patterns of rule. Global governance includes not only the actions of states and international institutions, but also the actions of non-governmental organizations (NGOs). It includes the markets and networks that emerge around many transnational issues. Global governance thus shifts attention from sovereign states in an anarchic international society to the creation, enforcement, and change of global patterns of activity.

Global governance also draws attention to the diverse objects that may be subject to rule in world politics. When realists and liberals concentrate on the anarchic nature of the international system, they imply that the more or less sole aim of international relations is to prevent war; the point of international institutions is to secure peace. In contrast, social scientists now suggest that global governance addresses diverse transnational problems. Global governance seeks not only to prevent and limit war but also to manage the global commons, to promote development, and to regulate global financial markets.

The theoretical lens of global governance has shifted the focus of social scientists from government as formal institutions towards governing as a complex set of processes and activities. This new focus is widespread. Even some realists use the broad idea of global governance to refer to anything that creates and enforces rules. Nonetheless, the broad idea of global governance remains controversial. Many realists still believe that the international system just is anarchic, so there can be no global governance. Proponents of global governance sometimes respond by arguing that older accounts of international relations are outdated. In this view social scientists have to turn to global governance if they are adequately to respond to changes in the world.

International institutions

'Global governance' can refer to changes in the world. The changes came at the end of the twentieth century. However, the early and mid-twentieth century witnessed numerous attempts to craft hierarchic and functional institutions to promote greater order, security, and justice in international affairs, and many of these institutions remain relevant today.

Many of the sources of the current form of global governance lie back in the late nineteenth and early twentieth century. One forerunner was a series of specialist agencies designed to manage transnational flows most notably in communications. The creation of specialized agencies to govern transnational issues stretches back at least to the middle of the nineteenth century. These agencies were strictly functional in design, and they regulated specific areas of concern. Early examples included the International Telegraphic Union (1865) and the Universal Postal Union (1874).

Other forerunners of global governance derive from liberalism. Liberal internationalists designed institutions to regulate the relations of states and so advance a perpetual peace and perhaps a just world. They hoped to enforce international law, arbitrate disputes, and regulate transnational trade by promoting both international institutions and political reform within states. Although liberal internationalism arguably had little impact on the practice of international relations until after the First World War, it then inspired the League of Nations along with attempts to implant liberal democratic regimes in the new states of Central and Eastern Europe.

Between the two world wars the specialized agencies were relatively successful in performing the functions for which they were designed. In contrast, the international institutions, particularly the League of Nations, glaringly failed to provide a forum for the peaceful resolution of disputes. Social scientists and policy-makers reacted to these experiences in ways that led to the foundations of today's international institutions. The League had relied on conference diplomacy combined with a commitment to collective security based on unanimity. Observers inferred that this approach could not uphold peace and security. Many turned to a more realist vision. The United Nations Security Council (UNSC) is the flawed fruit of their doing so—a collective international sovereign without a world state. Throughout the Cold War, it provided neither government nor governance.

Inter-war experiences encouraged liberal internationalists and their realist critics to look towards federalism, functionalism, and planning theory. Federalists argued that the problems of inter-state war and the unequal distribution of wealth required dramatic action. They called for the progressive creation of a world state by treaty, taking their inspiration from the federalism of the American Founding Fathers and Kant's essay on 'Perpetual Peace'. They feared that a war between the USA and the Soviet Union might result in a world state imposed by force. Their goal was thus to replace the anarchy of international relations with a world government.

The functionalists rejected both internationalism and federalism. They drew their inspiration from the practical experience and relative success of specialized agencies. In their view peaceful relations between states could emerge from functional agencies addressing discrete transnational problems. Functionalism promised peace by pieces; peace would arise as an effect of a series of agencies progressively reducing issues of conflict between states, turning political disputes into technical ones, and so binding states in ever closer relations.

Functionalism overlapped with sympathy for an increased role for planning in international relations. Enthusiasts argued that it was the absence of planning that had turned international relations in the first half of the twentieth century to anarchy. They wanted to replace the competition and conflict that they believed characterized classical liberalism with long-term thinking and rational planning. Technocratic planning would remove the insecurity and irrationality of the constant turmoil of free markets.

Internationalism, federalism, functionalism, and planning theory all contributed to international relations after the Second World War. As realist internationalism influenced the design of the UNSC, so a more general internationalism inspired the design of the UN General Assembly. Federalism influenced the European Economic Community, and the (not always successful) creation of postcolonial states with federal constitutions, such as Malaysia and Nigeria. The functionalist tradition also influenced the European Economic Community, and it helped to inspire various specialized agencies within and beyond the UN. Finally, planning theory influenced international, regional, state, and specialist actors, many of whom fused it with ideas emerging from the new field of development theory.

The post-war system of international relations confronted several problems in the 1970s. One problem was the rise of the South. The South questioned the legitimacy of the existing pattern of global governance. Its demands to redistribute wealth culminated in the Non-Aligned movement's 1973 proposal for a New International Economic Order. The Third World proved adept at using the UN to voice grievances about the attitude of particular states, especially the USA, to issues such as global trade and global finance. Parts of western opinion then became increasingly doubtful about the efficacy and desirability of international organization. Their doubts also fed on the paralysis of the UNSC during the Cold War.

Another problem of the 1970s was the falling apart of the Bretton Woods system for managing the global economy. The USA experienced inflationary pressures and worsening terms of trade.

Large amounts of dollars gathered in Europe and Japan. Foreign-held dollars lost their value. Inflation spread to other industrialized economies. In 1971 the USA ended the convertibility of the dollar into gold. Global exchange rate mechanisms collapsed. Although in 1973 the USA, the Europeans, and Japan agreed to formalize an arrangement in which their currencies floated freely in a deregulated market, this arrangement failed to restore stability and health to the global economy. Instead, the Gulf states increased the price of oil thereby aggravating the economic distress of the USA and Europe. The result was stagflation—a combination of high unemployment and high inflation.

Neoliberalism and globalization

By the late 1970s and early 1980s various problems had eroded the post-war consensus in the west about the best means of managing international relations and the global economy. Policy-makers responded to these problems by turning to a neoliberal emphasis on marketization and free trade.

Much neoliberalism reflects the critique of totalitarianism developed by scholars such as Friedrich Hayek. Hayek believed that planning and state action were inherently flawed. He argued that planners cannot know the subjective preferences of individuals, so they necessarily misallocate resources. Because planners cannot know and measure subjective preferences, they necessarily assign resources in accord with their particular perspectives and judgements, thus handing resources to special interests and spreading corruption. Neoliberals thus championed free markets as an alternative to planning. They argued that the state should not intervene in the economy, but merely uphold the rule of law and enable the market to work properly.

This neoliberalism came to dominate global financial institutions in the 1970s largely because of the powerful influence of the USA in forging what became known as the Washington Consensus. Neoliberals promoted market reforms and free trade by tying them to aid. In particular, the World Bank introduced structural adjustment loans tied to neoliberal policy reforms. Previously investment loans had been disbursed against project expenditures. The structural adjustment loans, in contrast, covered the costs associated with states' making the transition to more neoliberal economic policies, and they were paid out only as the states adopted neoliberal reforms.

In October 1985 the US Treasury Secretary, James Baker, proposed a plan that allowed developing states to restructure their debt in return for neoliberal reforms such as tax cuts, privatizing state-owned enterprises, reducing trade barriers, and liberalizing investment rules. Baker proposed, 'first, and foremost, the adoption by principal debtor countries of comprehensive macroeconomic and structural policies to promote growth and balance-of-payments adjustment to reduce inflation'. Mexico was the first nation to participate. It joined the General Agreement on Tariffs and Trade in 1986. By the end of 1988 it had reduced tariffs to a maximum of 20 per cent and to an average of 10 per cent. Mexico also undertook aggressive privatization; the number of state-owned enterprises dropped from 1,200 in 1982 to 500 in 1988. Later in March 1989 the then US Treasury Secretary, Nicholas Brady, announced a successor to Baker's plan. Although this Brady plan differed from its predecessor in many ways, it too used debt restructuring to promote neoliberal reforms.

Neoliberal policies faced much criticism, and in 1989 the World Bank shifted its emphasis from structural adjustment to good governance. The World Bank effectively recognized that economic reform alone could not secure development; political reform was required to stem corruption and misgovernment. By 2005 almost half of the conditions imposed on the recipients of loans concerned public sector governance.

At the same time as neoliberalism facilitated transnational exchanges, the end of the Cold War eroded the old bi-polar system of international security. These changes in economics and security combined to feed accounts of globalization.

Globalization is a complex and controversial idea. Although many social scientists use the term to refer to what they believe are growing transnational exchanges and dependencies, others remain sceptical. Still, many observers believe that there has been a significant increase in the flow of people, capital, goods, and information across borders. Many observers also believe that, partly as a result, various transnational policy problems have become increasingly important.

Initial studies of globalization concentrated on economic changes. Economists pointed to a rise in trade between states, the growing size and power of multinational corporations, and especially the increasing mobility of finance capital. Some economists now emphasize that globalization has been patchy. Globalization really encompasses Asia, Europe, and North America, and even within those areas, it is mainly evident in a few big cities. It bypasses much of the world including most of Africa.

More recent studies of globalization stretch to include non-economic policy issues such as the environment and security. Environmental issues have become more and more prominent. Many environmental issues are inherently global ones. Issues such as climate change cannot be addressed by isolated states; they require global action. Similarly, the growing focus on terrorist organizations means that security has become a more global, or at least transnational, problem for policy-makers. When terrorism is international, an effective response to it typically requires cooperation between the target country and the countries in which the terrorists are based. Further, terrorism can stem from failed states with endemic poverty and violent conflicts that lead some of their population to seek asylum elsewhere. These refugees are often yet another transnational problem.

Our global neighbourhood

Globalization seemed to have created a new world that required a new approach to governance. Indeed, although the term 'global governance' emerged in the late 1980s, it did not enter common usage until the late 1990s. Then the popularity of the term 'global governance' reflected a widespread belief that globalization and the collapse of the Soviet bloc had created a new world. The association of 'global governance' with this new world became clear with the publication of *Our Global Neighbourhood*.

In 1991 the UN set up a Commission on Global Governance. The Commission issued its report, *Our Global Neighbourhood*, in 1995. The report is especially important as it is one of the earliest usages of the term 'governance' in an international policy document. The report uses the word 'governance' to refer to an analytical lens on international affairs and a political agenda. Although the report offers a vision of global governance focused primarily on the UN, it also includes various new actors, particularly a new global civil society.

Our Global Neighbourhood spends some time outlining the forces eroding state sovereignty. It evokes 'a global flood of money, threats, images, and ideas [that] has overflowed the old system of national dikes that preserved state autonomy and control', before noting that 'pressure from illicit crossborder movements, and...political or economic developments could add to these flows'. Thus, although states remain the most important institutions for dealing with international issues, global governance includes 'non-governmental organizations...citizens' movements, multinational corporations...the global capital market [and]...global mass media'. To manage the interactions between all these new actors on the international stage, the report appeals to a 'global civil ethic' among political elites and the wider global population. Although the content of this ethic remains vague, the report implies that aspects of it already exist.

Here *Our Global Neighbourhood* reflects the optimism that policy-makers felt at the end of the Cold War. The report suggests that 'there is less ideological contention and less global confrontation in the world', and 'yet it is not a unipolar world, but a more plural one'. This plural world rests on and requires certain shared values. The report asserts boldly, 'there is a consensus that democracy, whatever form it may take, is a global entitlement, a right that should be available and protected for all', and 'the emergence of a global civil society is an important precondition of democracy at the global level'.

The report allows for non-state actors having an input to governance, but it focuses overwhelmingly on existing states and international institutions. Its vision is of top-down leadership legitimized by a civic ethos. The report calls for 'enlightened leadership to inspire people to acknowledge their responsibilities to each other and future generations'. It then complains that there is a 'dearth of leadership on major international issues'. The solution is for established leaders and institutions, especially the UN, to facilitate a change of culture within international relations.

According to *Our Global Neighbourhood*, the new world makes global institutions ever more important. The report insists that sovereignty must be exercised collectively if the world is to deal with not only the historic issues of conflict and security but also new issues such as managing the global commons. The report treats such issues in a uniform manner. It points to flaws in the current (usually ad hoc) system of governance only then to evoke the UN as the institution best capable of resolving these flaws.

Our Global Neighbourhood highlights the role of the UN in global affairs. It points to problems such as the lack of effective action on

UN resolutions and various unmitigated tragedies of the twentieth century that violated no treaty or international law because they lay within state boundaries. But the report then argues that the solution is to strengthen the UN. It calls for the expansion and improvement of international law and a stronger military force to improve the effectiveness of the UN as a peacekeeper.

Although *Our Global Neighbourhood* privileges the UN, it also takes a sanguine view of the ability of the free market to secure a bright future. A stronger UN will deal mainly with issues involving conflict and security. The market is adequate for most other issues. The report argues that globalization is creating greater economic interdependence among states, with a whole chapter on 'Managing Economic Interdependence'. It implies that current arrangements are inadequate to such interdependence. It suggests that the solution lies with fuller and freer markets. The role of international institutions such as the World Trade Organization is to protect weak states from bullying and to ensure that stronger states do not adopt protectionist policies.

A landmine story

The 1997 Ottawa Treaty, which is more formally known as 'The Convention on the Prohibition of the Use, Stockpiling, Production and Transfer of Anti-Personnel Mines and on their Destruction', aims to eliminate anti-personnel landmines. As of 2011 a total of 157 states are party to the Ottawa Treaty and a further two states have signed the Treaty but not ratified it; thirty-seven states have not signed it. The story of the treaty is an example of how NGOs can prompt states and work with them to create forms of global governance including formal international treaties.

Landmines are explosive devices that can be buried below ground and triggered by the weight of a person or vehicle passing over them. Their primary uses are defensive. They can create a barrier, making it hard for attacking forces to advance. They can create a kind of funnel, directing offensive forces to areas that are heavily defended. They can also just prevent enemy forces accessing and using an area that is considered to be of strategic value or to contain important resources. Whatever the intentions behind the use of landmines, they do not discriminate between combatants and non-combatants, and they remain deadly long after the end of the relevant conflict. Landmines are, in other words, especially vicious in their effects on innocent civilians.

Much the worst effects of landmines appear in developing states. One reason is that landmines were heavily used in the civil wars that have swept across much of Africa and parts of Asia. Further, the factions that planted these mines rarely kept a record of where they planted them, so it is often extremely difficult to remove them. The human effects of landmines are appalling, from death to loss of limb. The family effects often include not only the tragic death of loved ones but the also loss of income from the death or incapacitation of wage-earners. More generally still, landmines can seriously hamper efforts at economic development; they prevent the growth of agriculture, communities, and tourism.

It was the International Committee of the Red Cross that first drew global attention to landmines and their devastating impact. The Red Cross highlighted the dramatic rise in injuries caused by landmines in the 1980s. Other NGOs joined in the discussion. The various NGOs raised different types of concerns. Handicap International and Medico International focused on health issues. Human Rights Watch condemned the use of landmines as a violation of human rights. Although the NGOs phrased their concerns differently, they agreed on a single goal: landmines should be prohibited. The clarity and simplicity of this goal—and, I would like to add, its obvious good sense—attracted more groups, thereby further broadening the base of support. The result was an International Campaign to Ban Landmines (ICBL) in which over 1,200 NGOs participated.

The ICBL appeared to show an international civil society working across borders and drawing on diverse forms of expertise to educate and mobilize public opinion. Most states initially paid little attention to the issue of landmines. However, the ICBL proved adept at setting an agenda for states to discuss and then bringing that agenda to the forefront of public discussion. High-profile figures also helped publicize the cause. The most famous example was Diana, Princess of Wales, who in 1997 visited Angola where she walked through a minefield in a television spectacle that was broadcast worldwide. Around that time some governments began to pass laws that banned the use of landmines and strictly limited their manufacture.

Also at this time the ICBL was working with sympathetic states to create and institutionalize an international regime for dealing with landmines. Generally the NGOs provided an agenda and a degree of popular legitimacy to states such as Canada that were trying to pressurize more reluctant states such as the USA to commit to a new international treaty. A bottom-up version of the story presents the NGOs as the voice of world opinion, leading states and international organizations in what was effectively a new procedure for creating international law. A more statist version of the story suggests that sympathetic states effectively appealed to a selection of NGOs, and ignored others, in order to advance their agenda. Either way, a combination of NGOs and states led to the Ottawa Treaty and thereafter to annual votes in the UN General Assembly on resolutions proposing the universalization and full implementation of that Treaty.

The preamble to the Ottawa Treaty expresses the signatories' determination 'to put an end to the suffering and casualties caused by anti-personnel mines, that kill or maim hundreds of people every week, mostly innocent and defenceless civilians and especially children, obstruct economic development and reconstruction, inhibit the repatriation of refugees and internally displaced persons, and have other severe consequences'. The states who sign the treaty commit themselves never 'to use anti-personnel mines', 'to develop, produce, otherwise acquire, stockpile, retain or transfer to anyone, directly or indirectly, anti-personnel mines', or 'to assist, encourage or induce, in any way, anyone to engage in any activity prohibited to a State Party under this Convention'.

A new world order

Globalization consists in the rise of transnational flows and transnational problems. Social scientists often argue that globalization has changed the nature and role of the state. The state is no longer the sole arbiter of what occurs within its borders. Whether states like it or not, they increasingly have to address supra-territorial issues, actors, and interests. In addition, globalization occurred alongside a shift in the circumstances and uses of war. Inter-state conflicts are less common, and intra-state conflicts are more widespread. Finally, as states tried to exercise control over a rapidly changing world, they created new multilateral regulatory arrangements. The overall result of globalization is thus a more multilayered and privatized system of governance. Multilayered governance involves regulation by sub-state, state, and supra-state bodies with transborder connections at each layer. Privatized governance includes business groups, NGOs, and arguably organized crime.

As neoliberalism began to falter or at least lose some of its initial confidence, so policy-makers tried to govern this new world order through networks as much as markets. Revised versions of functionalism and planning theory reasserted themselves. New forms of social science led people both to notice the increasing role of networks and actively to foster new types of partnership among states and between states and other actors. This return to planning theory and functionalism reflects the experiences and

THE Thought Leadership Conference

THE WHOLE OF GOVERNMENT APPROACH TO HOMELAND SECURITY AND DEFENSE

5. The terrorist attacks of 9/11 led many policy-makers to turn to whole-of-government approaches to security, fragile states, and development aid

dilemmas of the 1990s and after. New dilemmas relating to terrorism, climate change, asylum seekers, and the digital divide appear to be less about efficiency than about collective goods such as security and equity. Other dilemmas have risen as unintended consequences of neoliberalism itself.

Recent shifts in global governance reflect the turn to networks, joining-up, and public–private partnerships. One prominent example is international aid to fragile states. Development agencies have changed partly because they have been tasked with a novel role in promoting security. Development agencies are now a first line of defence for western societies in fear of mass migration, transnational crime, and terrorist networks. Before 9/11 debates about aid were conducted mainly in terms of the economic needs of underdeveloped states. Since the terrorist attacks greater attention has been paid to fragile states and the wicked problems that they confront. Fragile states are defined not just by poverty but also by related problems of weak governance and violent conflict.

The shift from hierarchy to markets and networks has altered the ways in which development agencies operate. From the mid-1990s onwards development agencies have been transformed from top-down fully integrated service providers into facilitators that seek to steer and oversee complex networks composed of public, voluntary, and private sector actors. Britain's Department for International Development was formed explicitly to foster networks: the 1997 White Paper on International Development saw the critical task as developing partnerships with other government agencies, various actors in target countries, NGOs at home and abroad, and scholarly researchers. Similarly, in 1999 in the aftermath of the Kosovo conflict US AID funded or subcontracted its activities to an international public organization, twelve American NGOs, and five local NGOs. The situation in Afghanistan is even more complex.

International aid to fragile states typically tries now to address wicked problems through networks. Donor states increasingly conceive of effective aid as dependent on a whole-of-government approach that sets out to address all these problems simultaneously. They argue that effective aid to fragile states depends on networks that combine actors and issues associated with foreign policy, security, and development. By 2005 Australia, Germany, the UK, and the USA had established units dedicated to coordinating the efforts of various departments involved in the reconstruction of fragile states. Several states were exploring novel funding arrangements to encourage greater interdepartmental collaboration.

The international community as a whole appears to be moving towards support for a whole-of-government approach to aid more generally. From February to March 2005 a high-level forum on Joint Progress Toward Enhanced Aid Effectiveness met in Paris. The forum brought together over a hundred countries as well as international institutions such as the African Development Bank, the Asian Development Bank, the European Bank for Reconstruction and Development, the Organization for Economic Cooperation and Development, the World Bank, and the UN Development Programme. The forum resulted in the Paris Declaration, which called for greater harmonization and alignment and for managing aid in relation to a set of indicators.

Global governance now includes numerous such attempts to coordinate diverse actors within markets and networks. International institutions such as the UN and EU have created new bodies, often themselves networks or partnerships, to try to regulate and control transnational affairs. Similarly, there has been a growth of informal networks among other actors such as high court judges and special representatives. In 2009 the USA appointed the veteran diplomat Richard Holbrooke as a Special Representative to help coordinate intra-government action on Afghanistan and Pakistan. Other states, including Australia, Britain, and France, soon followed suit. Initially these special representatives formed a small contact group, but before the end of 2010 their number had grown to the point where they constituted a rather large and arguably unwieldy committee.

Has globalization with its transnational flows and transnational problems really created a new world order of complex institutions, markets, and networks involving public, voluntary, and private sector actors? Debates about the extent to which we live in a new world of global governance often echo those about the changing role of the state in public governance. Indeed, much of the literature on global governance develops or reacts against accounts of globalization and its impact on the state. Some social scientists draw on the idea that globalization has weakened the state to expand the scope of international relations beyond the analysis of states and international institutions. These social scientists concentrate on the rules of global governance and the authority of those that make and enforce them.

Other social scientists react against the claims that globalization has weakened the state. They argue that states are still sovereign powers, so the rise of multilayered and private governance does not signal a significant transformation in international relations. They think of the new global governance as a product of states adopting new means to secure the same old ends. In this view non-state actors have not displaced states; rather, they are the tools of states. Strong states still cajole weak ones into complying with their preferences, and these strong states only delegate regulatory authority to non-state actors when it suits their interests. The strong states retain final control. They just devolve the day-to-day activities of regulation and regime management to other actors.

Yet other social scientists offer critical versions of the idea of a new global governance. They do not deny that international relations have changed. They just argue that the changes are products of, for example, global capitalism, western self-interest, or neoliberalism. They stress the interdependence of global governance, the agendas of the main global financial institutions, and neoliberal and neoconservative policies. Many of the critics also discuss sources of resistance to global governance; they look especially to social movements in a nascent global civil society.

So, social scientists paint three rather different portraits of the new world of global governance. Some argue that globalization has radically reshaped states and institutions and also introduced new actors. Others argue that traditional actors have simply begun to use new modes of governance to advance their long-standing goals and interests. Yet others argue that any such changes have given control of global governance to actors with agendas detrimental to global welfare.

Chapter 6
Good governance

Irrespective of the extent of the shift from government to governance, the spread of governance theory and related ideas certainly posed new problems and inspired new agendas. Governance agendas address problems of efficiency, development, capacity, accountability, and legitimacy. They try to combine practical effectiveness with ethical (mainly liberal democratic) values. Some agendas are presented as more or less universal panaceas that allegedly apply at all times and in all places. Others are presented as more specific responses to new times and practices associated with globalization, information technology, and the new governance itself. All these agendas are attempts to promote competing visions of good governance, although the actual term 'good governance' gets used most often to refer narrowly to development strategies.

Unsurprisingly governance agendas have followed the same loose trajectory as corporate, public, and global governance from hierarchy through markets to networks. The nineteenth century privileged the ideals of representative government. In the early twentieth century social scientists and policy-makers increasingly appealed in addition to a responsible bureaucracy as a necessary counter to the factionalism and irrationalism of much democratic politics. In the late twentieth century, faith in bureaucracy gave way to faith in markets and networks. Yet, insofar as markets and networks too seem to be failing, perhaps we should look instead to more collaborative and participatory forms of governance.

Representative and responsible government

The classic meaning of good democratic government emphasizes representative and responsible institutions. These ideals flourished in the nineteenth and early twentieth centuries. Representative legislatures facilitated self-rule in large societies. Responsible bureaucracies allowed neutral experts to guide public policy as a counterbalance to party factionalism. Although these ideals still resonate, they have limited fit to the new theories and practices of governance.

A representative democracy has citizens of a state exercising popular sovereignty through legitimately elected representatives. In a representative democracy the citizens choose their representatives by voting in elections. Typically the chosen representatives congregate in a legislative assembly where they debate policy and determine legislation. The classical theory of representative democracy suggests that the representatives act in accord with the will or interests of the citizens. The representatives are not simply proxies for the citizens; rather, they have considerable discretion to support the policies that they believe will most benefit their constituents. Nonetheless, because the role of the representatives is at least in part to act on behalf of their constituents, it is important that the voters have a way of holding them accountable. Accountability has generally been tied to transparency and periodic elections. Transparency enables the citizens to keep track of the actions of their representatives. Periodic elections enable the citizens to replace their representatives should they be unhappy with the actions of their representatives.

The classical theory of representative democracy broadly supposed that elected politicians would act in accord with the will and interests of their constituents. This supposition has been increasingly questioned. For a start, various interest groups play a powerful and even dominant role in the policy process. Corporate interests in particular use their extensive resources to become powerful lobbyists, financiers, and advisers to politicians. The worry is that powerful interests can lead political representatives to act, whether intentionally or not, on behalf of particular elites rather than the general public. In addition, the sheer complexity of modern societies threatens many of the ideals of representative democracy. If the classic theory implied that public policy was made by elected representatives in a transparent manner, not much of that account remains today. Even when legislatures pass statutes, the statutes are often vague and their interpretation, application, and enforcement falls to administrative and judicial bodies that possess the relevant technical expertise. Further, the technical issues involved in many laws and policies entail a loss of transparency. Few citizens have the appropriate legal and scientific knowledge to evaluate the laws and policies.

Early in the twentieth century social scientists, such as Mosei Ostrogrorski and Graham Wallas, drew attention to factionalism, propaganda, financial extravagances, and other problems in representative democracies. The ideal of a responsible bureaucracy spread in part as a response to these problems. The bureaucracy was meant to provide a bulwark against the irrationalities of the electorate and their representatives. It was meant in addition to prevent organized interests taking control of public policy. A permanent and neutral bureaucracy would divide politics from policy. Public policy would be legitimate because it would be based on science. Elected representatives would define policy goals and check the activity of experts. Social scientists, professionals, and generalist civil servants would use their expertise to devise rational scientific policies in accord with these goals.

Bureaucracy appealed as a way of preserving representative democracy while removing its worst features—instability, irrationality, and factionalism—from the day-to-day activities of governing. Of course, policy can never be separated entirely from politics. When social scientists championed responsible bureaucracy, they did not usually think that was a literal description of how public servants operated; rather, they thought of it as an ideal type enshrining a commitment to certain values. They associated bureaucracy with public spirit and scientific neutrality defined in stark contrast to the self-interest and factionalism found in democratic processes. Some of them also associated bureaucracy with efficiency; bureaucracy was a rational form of organization that facilitated specialization according to function.

Development theory

The new governance arose as hierarchic organization fell out of favour and social scientists and policy-makers began to look to

OF **COURSE** YOU DON'T WANT TO BE HOMELESS AND MALNOURISHED, I MEAN **WHO WOULD,** BUT YOU SEE WE **HAD** TO STRUCTURALLY ADJUST YOUR COUNTRY OR YOU'D HAVE ENDED UP MISSING OUT ON ECONOMIC GROWTH, AND THEN YOU'D BE IN A RIGHT OLD MESS, WOULDN'T YOU, BECAUSE **ONE DAY** THAT ECONOMIC GROWTH IS GOING TO TRICKLE DOWN TO **YOU,** YOU SEE, AND SO **YOUR** PARENTS LOSING THEIR JOBS AND THE PRICE OF FOOD DOUBLING IS **ACTUALLY** A JOLLY GOOD THING, REALLY... ISN'T IT? ...EH?

IMF

6. **Structural adjustment loans, and the neoliberal theories that inspired them, were always extremely contentious**

markets and networks as alternatives to bureaucracy. The main impetus for this shift to markets and networks was the notion that they would improve organizational and inter-organizational efficiency. Nonetheless, the shift raised the question of whether or not markets and networks fitted with representative democracy as neatly as had the ideal of a responsible bureaucracy. Some neoliberals tried to initiate a rather different discussion by arguing that markets did more than democracy to advance the values of individual choice and freedom. The main public policy debate was, however, about the relationship of markets and networks to liberal and democratic institutions. This debate was most explicit in discussions of development.

Discussions of good governance in development combined theoretical and policy-oriented strands. The theoretical strand concerned the relations between the state and a democratic civil society; it concentrated on the ways in which power and authority impact on development. The policy-oriented strand concerned the relations between the state and the market; it concentrated on the ways in which the effectiveness of economic aid by donors varies with the institutional arrangements in the recipient state. These theoretical and policy-oriented strands came together in a liberal view of development, according to which liberal democratic institutions help protect market freedoms and combat corruption thereby promoting development and increasing the effectiveness of aid.

Liberal democratic governance thus got presented as a prerequisite of successful economic development. Sometimes definitions of good governance had a narrow focus on competitive elections, clear lines of accountability, and the rule of law. Other definitions spread out more broadly to include pluralism, respect for human rights, and a broad base of political participation.

Whereas 'good governance' rarely entered debates about development prior to the late 1980s, it then became an integral part of scholarly theories and policy agendas. In 1989 the World Bank published a report, *Sub-Saharan Africa: From Crisis to Sustainable Growth*, that evoked a 'crisis of governance' as a key underlying barrier to development in much of Africa. The World Bank began to use the term 'good governance' to cover both technical areas and civil society. The technical areas included legal frameworks for development (consistent laws, an independent judiciary, and the place in codified law of concepts such as fairness, justice, and liberty) and capacity-building (better policy analysis, stricter budgetary discipline, and public service reforms). The concern with civil society included legitimacy, transparency, accountability, and participation, all of which were presented as ways of strengthening civil society, reducing the power of the state, attacking corruption, and ensuring the efficient allocation of public resources. The same ends also led the World Bank to promote strong local government and decentralized administration.

Discussions of good governance and development have continued to change in subtle and not so subtle ways. One important change followed a growing concern with failed states, which seemed to be the main bases for transnational terrorists. Some social scientists argue that the earlier development policies of the World Bank aggravated the problems confronting failed states. Because failed states suffer from being too weak effectively to implement their policies, development policies that seek to reduce the power of the state, promote decentralization, and strengthen social actors are counter-productive. This view inspires an emphasis on building state institutions and state capacity. The key aim is to improve the ability of the state to oversee, regulate, and steer the networks of actors now involved in development. Specific policies often include the education and training of public sector workers, the establishment of management systems, and the promotion of networks among the relevant stakeholders.

106

Democratic worries

A curious optimism pervaded many of the early discussions of the democratic potential of the new governance. The optimism over markets reflected a kind of liberal triumphalism following the collapse of the Soviet bloc. The optimism over networks also reflected a more general sense that the end of the Cold War provided a chance to forge a new agenda, address problems that had been sidelined, correct flaws in institutions, and meet emerging challenges. Governance thus embodied hopes for a free and vibrant civil society. The hope was that democracy could bubble up from below with civil society defending the rights of the oppressed and underrepresented against otherwise overpowering vested interests.

This optimism appeared, for example, in *Our Global Neighbourhood*—the report of the Commission on Global Governance. The report contrasted the democratic potential of global governance with the possible dangers of a concentration of power under global government. The authors of the report wrote, 'we are not proposing movement towards a world government, for were we to travel in that direction we could find ourselves in an even less democratic world than we have—one more accommodating to power, more hospitable to hegemonic ambition, and more reinforcing of the roles of states and governments rather than the rights of people'. The report looked instead to new forms of global governance to nurture a global civic ethic, strengthen global security, manage economic interdependence, reform the United Nations, and bolster the rule of law in international relations. It wanted to involve 'non-governmental organizations...citizens' movements, multinational corporations, and the global capital market'. The existing system of international institutions remained central, but the focus was on 'improving its means of collaboration with private and independent groups'.

Today most observers are less optimistic about the democratic potential of network governance. There are two main concerns.

The first is that the complexity of networks seems to undermine important democratic values including, most prominently, accountability. Classic accounts of accountability rely on clearly defined offices arranged in an unbroken line of command that reaches up to elected politicians. The involvement of diverse actors in policy-making and service delivery blurs lines of accountability. It is increasingly difficult to say who exactly should be held responsible for what. The involvement of a multiplicity of organizations with overlapping jurisdictions means that the pattern of service provision can be difficult to discern. The state may be able to cancel its contracts with private and voluntary sector actors, but these actors are rarely part of a chain of authority that ends with voters. Further, because public officials are increasingly meant to be more entrepreneurial and to operate outside the bureaucracy and its rules, even they are not always subject to clear lines of accountability.

A second concern is that when policy actors introduce network governance as a top-down project, they are often more interested in efficiency gains and in building their legitimacy than in empowering citizen participation. Policy elites generally promote networks as yet another turn in the cycle of modernism. Experts tell them that networks increase coordination, build social capital, and contribute to government legitimacy. The policy elites then adopt network governance as a technocratic means to efficiency. The European Union (EU) White Paper on Governance explicitly began with effectiveness as the rationale for citizen involvement: 'the quality, relevance and effectiveness of EU policies depend on ensuring participation throughout the policy chain—from conception to implementation.' In practice this focus on efficiency gains means that state actors try to retain control of the networks. Participation becomes incorporation. Further, when the state loses control of the networks or when the networks do not act as the central state wishes, then the centre often resorts to targets and terror as a means of trying to direct the networks.

Collaborative governance

Growing doubts about the democratic credentials of network governance are beginning to lead some social scientists and policy-makers to explore more innovative forms of collaborative governance. Collaborative governance can be defined broadly to make it closely resemble network governance; it refers here to any attempt to create and conduct policy that involves sustained participation by public and voluntary sector actors. Yet, collaborative governance can also be defined more narrowly in order to distinguish it more sharply from network governance; it refers here to attempts to bring all the relevant stakeholders together for face-to-face discussions during which policies are developed.

Collaborative governance refers mainly to cases in which citizens play a more active role in policy-making or service delivery. The actors from civil society who are interested in a policy play an active role in the policy process from initial discussions over the agenda to completion. Examples of the relevant social actors include not only businesses, unions, and non-governmental organizations, but also citizen groups of, for example, local residents. Typically collaborative governance is an interactive process in which myriad actors with various interests, perspectives, and knowledge are brought together. Collaborative governance differs from network governance, therefore, because it involves the citizens affected by a policy or service, not just private or voluntary sector organizations with which the state forms a contract or partnership. Again, collaborative governance differs from whole-of-government approaches because it brings citizens' groups into the policy-making process, not just diverse government departments and agencies.

Obviously collaborative governance can still blur lines of accountability. Also, it may give more weight to the opinions and interests of social actors who get involved than those who do not.

Equally, however, collaborative governance appears to promote other democratic values, including participation and dialogue, both of which are rather neglected by representative institutions. Collaborative governance thus holds out the possibility that improved participation and dialogue can fill the gaps that have appeared in the ideals and practices of representative and responsible government.

Collaborative innovations can be found throughout the policy cascade from public opinion formation through decision-making to policy implementation. Innovations in public opinion formation include attempts to build mini-publics that deliberate on policy issues. Examples include town-hall meetings, deliberative polls, and consensus conferences, all of which seek to improve the quality of public opinion through open discussion. Other innovations focus on trying to get citizens and especially marginalized groups to learn about the social world and think critically about their place in it. Various forms of participatory learning encourage citizens themselves to decide the purposes of research enquiry.

Other innovations bear more on decision-making processes. Referenda are a long-standing way of enabling citizens to play an active role in particular decisions. In recent years, however, there has been an upsurge in the use of other participatory technologies including citizens' assemblies and participatory budgeting. In 1996 the Indian state of Kerala launched a 'People's Campaign for Decentralized Planning'. This Campaign gave new resources and functions to the state's local governments including discretionary budgeting authority over 35–40 per cent of the state's total development expenditures. The local governments were then charged with designing and implementing their own development plans through a sequence of participatory meetings in which citizens would have a direct role in shaping projects and policies.

Typically participatory budgeting and decentralized development planning also give citizens an active role in implementing policies.

Kerala's Campaign encouraged local organizations to implement public works through committees of project beneficiaries rather than contractors. Other innovations in policy implementation have arisen alongside the new governance and the proliferation of markets and networks. Sometimes the beneficiaries have become coproducers in the creation of the goods that they consume or in the management of the services they use. When the state withdraws—entirely or in part—from the direct provision of certain goods and services, space for democratic innovations sometimes emerges and substantial forms of citizen self-organization sometimes take root.

An irrigation story

Although Taiwan has a plentiful supply of water, the supply is uneven, with most of the water supply falling in a short rainy season. Effective year-round farming depends on irrigation. The land reforms in the 1950s created a system in which most Taiwanese farmers own only small parcels of land. Effective irrigation depends on coordination and organization among numerous farmers. For the system to run smoothly, farmers need to work together and follow the water allocation rules, and maintain their system and structure. The governance of water is crucial yet complex.

Taiwan's current water management system is a form of collaborative governance. The government created the system and continues to supervise it. Also, although the farmers fund the system by paying water fees, the central government has been paying a lot of the water fees on their behalf since the 1990s. It is, however, the farmers who maintain and operate the system through the irrigation associations, which they own and operate. The farmers' representatives in the irrigation associations and local irrigation groups decide where and how the water fees are spent.

Farmers in relatively close proximity form irrigation associations, and it is these associations that operate and manage the irrigation system. The irrigation associations serve multiple purposes. They help to reduce the amount of time individual farmers have to spend on water management issues. They also help to limit conflicts among farmers over uneven rates of participation. Indeed, as the whole water management system depends so heavily on collaboration among the famers, one crucial role of the irrigation associations is to foster trust and solidarity among farmers. The whole water management system rests on ordered and respectful relationships among the farmers and between the farmers and the irrigation associations.

Irrigation associations have both a headquarters and field offices. The individual famers elect representatives who oversee the irrigation association. These representatives elect a chairman who sits atop the organizational headquarters. The chairman appoints the general manager and chief engineer who oversee the daily affairs of the association.

The headquarters are responsible for overall planning, large-scale maintenance, management of water sources, and water delivery at the system level. The field offices are the heavy-lifters of the system. Their main tasks are to collect the information on which overall plans are based, to oversee local planning, to deal with local disputes, and to distribute water to individual farmers. The field stations include both local officials and local irrigation groups made up of farmers. The field stations are thus the main sites at which individual farmers interact with irrigation associations.

Field offices have local autonomy. They include both management and working stations. The management stations collect the information needed to plan irrigation, and they manage the implementation of the resulting plans. The working stations concentrate on daily operations. Although they are not formally involved in decision-making processes, they provide insights into how the system is functioning and tips on how to improve it.

Most field offices are small, containing some seven to ten officials. They are flexible and their working environment is informal. Because they have to be ready to respond at any moment if there is an emergency, the station chief usually lives on site. The field offices have close contact with the local farmers. Individual officials at the station are responsible for particular geographic areas and they work closely with the relevant farmers. The officials are held individually responsible for what happens in their particular areas, but there is also close cooperation among the officials because they are held collectively responsible should anything go wrong within the field office as a whole. The local officials and the leaders of the farmers' irrigation groups are usually members of the local community.

Every year, at the start of planting season, local officials and irrigation groups meet to plan irrigation operations for that year. The main issue is usually the estimated demand for the season. Estimates of demand reflect cropping patterns and field geography. The working stations cooperate with the farmers to compile information about the farmers' demands. This information goes to the irrigation associations' headquarters. If the estimated demand exceeds the amount of available water, the association has to decide which areas will get how much water. The resulting irrigation plan is very detailed. Water delivery itself is, however, the responsibility of the working stations.

So, the farmers' representatives in the irrigation groups vouch for the amount of water the farmers need. The irrigation association then determines the amount of water to be given to each local group. It is then up to the farmers themselves, through their local irrigation groups, to decide how to allocate the water among the relevant farms. Local officials and irrigation groups develop plans for how much water each farm receives. The working stations follow these detailed plans. They employ 'water guards' to carry out the water allocation plans.

Water is an entitlement of the farmers. The irrigation plans serve as a means by which the farmers can evaluate the performance of the irrigation associations and field offices so as to hold them accountable. Farmers who are part of the irrigation association are automatically members of their local irrigation group. They participate in its meetings and they vote for its leaders about once every four years. Typically, however, it is only the leaders and members of the irrigation groups who actively participate. Further, even the local officials often play only a small role in the affairs of the irrigation associations' headquarters. Conflicts are usually between farmers who are high and low in a water channel. Theft remains a problem, but research suggests that the irrigation associations, with their collaborative system of governance, have made it less severe.

Assessing governance

'Good governance'—like 'corporate governance', 'public governance', 'global governance', and 'governance' more generally—has served three main purposes. It has recast theoretical perspectives. It has highlighted seemingly new practices. And it has set agendas for change.

Governance as *theory* decentres the corporation, the state, and the international system. It reminds people—for unless they have been bewitched by modernist social science, surely they know this—that corporations, states, and systems do not exist apart from the people and actions of which they are composed. Governance as theory prompts people to pay less attention to allegedly fixed institutions and more to shifting processes. It reminds people—for surely this too is part of everyday knowledge—that institutions are made up of individuals who act on their personal and perhaps conflicting beliefs and desires.

This theoretical shift is, in my view, all to the good. Indeed, I think that we should extend the insights of governance theory even further. Corporations, states, and systems do not have intrinsic logics and properties that make it inevitable that they will act in a particular way to produce a particular outcome. On the contrary, institutions are open practices that people are constantly creating, modifying, and transforming through their actions as these too change in response to all kinds of unforeseen circumstances. Social life does not, in my view, fit neatly into modernist categories, schemas, and formal explanations. Social life is inherently messy and permanently in flux.

Governance as *new practices* suggests that since the late 1970s there has been a shift from hierarchies to markets and especially networks. It suggests that globalization and public sector reforms have given rise to hybrid and multi-jurisdictional practices of governing in which public, voluntary, and private actors work together in networks and partnerships. The state is a less important actor, constrained by its dependence on others. Instead of dictating policy and commanding other actors, the state has to negotiate with other actors and use metagovernance strategies to steer them.

Claims about the new governance are, in my view, difficult to assess. Much of the difficulty lies in untangling the relationship between the new practices and governance as theory. It is probable that governance theory (and related ideas) has led people to see the world differently. To some extent, therefore, the new practices of governance are less new states of affairs than a new recognition of old states of affairs. The state never was a unified entity capable of imposing its will on society. The state has always had to negotiate with other policy actors, build trust among them, and use diplomacy to steer them. Networks have always been prevalent throughout public policy. Non-governmental actors have always played active roles in international relations. In short, government has long been about governance; it is just that many people did not realize it.

It also seems clear that various strands of modernist social science and related ideas have inspired some policy-makers actively to promote new practices. A growing dissatisfaction with bureaucracy led corporations, states, and others to look to alternative forms of organization. Neoclassical economics, principal–agent theory, and neoliberalism played a role in policy-makers introducing privatization, contracting-out, marketization, and a new public management. Likewise, institutionalism, network theory, and planning theory, with its idea of wicked problems, contributed to the fashion for joining-up and whole-of-government approaches. In short, different policy actors have tried to create new practices of governance; it is just unclear how successful they have been.

The remaining issue is, therefore, whether changes in society and public policy have transformed governance. My own view is that there has been a transformation. States have both become less powerful and adopted new strategies. However, it is easy to overstate the extent of this transformation, especially if one fails to recognize the extent to which new theories have led us to see the world differently. Transnational flows have increased, but they were always present. States have forged new types of contracts and partnerships with other actors, but they have long formed and implemented policy in ways that involve other actors. Corporations have modified their systems of executive compensation and become more conscious of their place in society, but the changes are uneven and, especially in the case of social responsibility, often paid little more than lip-service.

A democratic future

Governance *agendas* have generally privileged markets and networks over hierarchies. They have thereby undermined the values associated with representative and responsible government. Decisions are regularly made not by elected representatives but by unelected officials and non-governmental actors. Accountability is a fiction that few people believe in enough to try to make it work. It might seem, therefore, as if our democratic ideals are losing their relevance to the world in which we live. Fortunately, however, collaborative governance points towards a new democratic agenda in which participation and dialogue supplement representation and accountability.

For many, the justification for collaborative governance might be primarily an ethical one. Collaborative governance can advance the democratic ideal of self-rule. It can expand the range and depth of opportunities available to citizens to participate in decisions that affect them and those they care about. Having the opportunity to defend one's beliefs and interests or those of others through political participation is a freedom to which democrats attach great value. However, collaborative governance has not only to meet widely shared democratic values but also to be effective. Even if collaborative innovations are of value in themselves, the relevant constituencies also need to believe that these innovations will 'work'.

Some empirical studies suggest that collaborative governance, with its emphasis on participation and dialogue among citizens, can improve the effectiveness of the policy process. Service quality is one important part of good governance. But service quality is difficult to assess. One approach is simply to ask citizens and officials to give their own assessments of it. Using this approach, Kerala's Campaign for Decentralized Planning appears to have worked well. The main evidence comes from a survey of seventy-two *panchayats* (village councils). This survey asked respondents whether the quality of services and development had improved, deteriorated, or stayed the same in each of thirteen categories. A notable majority of the respondents felt that there had been either 'some' or 'significant' improvement for all of the thirteen categories. When social scientists disaggregated the data according to the role of the respondent (e.g. ruling politician, opposition politician, public official, and civil society actor), the overall positive evaluation of the Campaign's impact remained; for all thirteen categories, a majority of each type of respondent felt that there had been improvement.

It would be foolish to suggest that collaborative arrangements are a panacea for all the ills of modern governance. Difficult problems require a reliance on participation and dialogue as supplements to representation and accountability. One major problem is that rates of participation in many forms of collaborative governance strongly favour the wealthy, the more educated, and those who belong to dominant racial and ethnic groups.

Nonetheless, the key point, in my opinion, is that collaborative governance might break with the cycle of modernism. Modernist social science appears to offer a formal expertise into the more or less intrinsic properties of various types of organization and other social phenomena. All too often policy-makers come to believe that if they promote a particular type of organization or even a particular policy, it will more or less inevitably produce certain results. Modern governance has thus been heavily informed by the formal expertise and ideal types of modernist social science— hierarchy, market, and network. In sharp contrast, collaborative governance seems to involve a rejection of formal expertise in favour of dialogue and interaction with citizens.

A rejection of modernist social science and its ideal types would facilitate a greater attention to the context and specificity of policy issues and their solutions. When policy-makers and democratic organizations attempt to promote a particular collaborative practice in dissimilar contexts, widely different outcomes might emerge. More often than not, the outcomes will include some that members of the democratic organization would like to modify. Sometimes they might be able to modify these outcomes by tinkering with the relevant collaborative arrangements. There are, for example, strategies for increasing the participation in collaborative practices of marginalized communities, the poor, and the under-educated. One strategy is selective recruitment: a participatory forum can be open to all and yet its organizers can make explicit efforts to recruit participants from certain groups. Another such strategy is random selection: the organizers of a participatory forum can deliberately select participants from the general population to ensure they reflect the groups within it. Of course, sometimes democratic organizations might conclude that the drawbacks of participatory and dialogic practices outweigh their benefits. There may be occasions, for example, when a move towards collaborative governance of environmental resources leads to their degradation. In such cases, policy-makers need to weigh the values advanced by collaborative practices against those they might undercut.

The new governance still tries to supplement representative government with modernist expertise; it just favours an expert faith in markets and networks over one in hierarchic bureaucracy. Collaborative governance provides an alternative in which modernist expertise gives way to participation and dialogue. Democratic organizations can become ongoing experiments in which the members collaboratively solve their collective problems and manage their collective affairs not in accord with the ideal types of modernist social science but by engaging with one another. Democracy can create the knowledge necessary to improve governance.

Further reading

Chapter 1: What is governance?

Introductory texts on governance include V. Chottray and G. Stoker, *Governance Theory: A Cross-Disciplinary Approach* (Basingstoke: Palgrave, 2010); A.-M. Kjaer, *Governance* (Cambridge: Polity, 2004); and J. Pierre and B. Peters, *Governance, Politics and the State* (Basingstoke: Macmillan 2000). For more detailed and advanced coverage of the main topics covered by the governance literature see M. Bevir, ed., *The SAGE Handbook of Governance* (London: Sage, 2011); and M. Salamon, ed., *The Tools of Government: A Guide to the New Governance* (New York: Oxford University Press, 2002). The classic argument for a unified sovereign state is Thomas Hobbes, *Leviathan*, ed. R. Tuck (Cambridge: Cambridge University Press, 1996). On the rise of this concept of the state see Q. Skinner, *The Foundations of Modern Political Thought* (Cambridge: Cambridge University Press, 1978). For later nineteenth- and twentieth-century pluralist challenges to it see J. Bartelson, *The Critique of the State* (Cambridge: Cambridge University Press, 2001); J. Gunnell, *Imagining the American Polity: Political Science and the Discourse of Democracy* (University Park, Pa.: Pennsylvania State University Press, 2004); and D. Runciman, *Pluralism and the Personality of the State* (Cambridge: Cambridge University Press, 2005). I am grateful to Dr Caitriona Carter for allowing me to use her research to tell the aquaculture story. She will publish part of it in C. Carter, 'Integrating Sustainable Development in the European Government of Industry: Sea Fisheries and Agriculture Compared', in N. Shuibhne and

L. Gormley, eds., *From Single Market to Economic Union* (Milton Keynes: Open University Press, 2012).

Chapter 2: Organizational governance

A good introduction to organization theory is M. Hatch with A. Cunliffe, *Organization Theory: Modern, Symbolic, and Postmodern Perspectives* (Oxford: Oxford University Press, 2006). A particularly relevant set of readings is G. Thompson, J. Frances, R. Levacic, and J. Mitchell, eds., *Markets, Hierarchies, and Networks: The Coordination of Social Life* (London: Sage, 1991). For more historical approaches see R. Denhardt, *Theories of Public Organization* (Belmont, Calif.: Wadsworth, 2010); and J. Tompkins, *Organization Theory and Public Management* (Belmont, Calif.: Wadsworth, 2004). Max Weber's classic study of bureaucracy is in M. Weber, *The Theory of Social and Economic Organization*, trans. A. Henderson and T. Parsons (London: Macmillan, 1947). Much of Herbert Simon's work draws on ideas he first expressed in H. Simon, *Administrative Behavior: A Study of Decision-Making Processes in Administrative Organizations* (New York: Free Press, 1947). Interesting advanced studies include D. Chisholm, *Coordination without Hierarchy: Informal Structures in Multiorganizational Systems* (Berkeley and Los Angeles: University of California Press, 1989); J. Hassard, *Sociology and Organization Theory: Positivism, Paradigms, and Postmodernity* (Cambridge: Cambridge University Press, 1993); and O. Williamson, *The Mechanisms of Governance* (New York: Oxford University Press, 1996). On markets and networks also see, respectively, C. Lindblom, *The Market System: What It Is, How It Works, and What to Make of It* (New Haven: Yale University Press, 2001); and M. Kilduff and W. Tasi, *Social Networks and Organizations* (Thousand Oaks, Calif.: Sage, 2003). I discuss the impact of social science on changing worlds of governance in M. Bevir, *Democratic Governance* (Princeton: Princeton University Press, 2010).

Chapter 3: Corporate governance

The literature on corporate governance is vast. Good starting places include C. Mallin, *Corporate Governance* (Oxford: Oxford University Press, 2009); and R. Monks and N. Minow, *Corporate Governance* (Oxford: Blackwell Publishers, 2001). For a more specific focus on the Board of Directors and the Chief Executive Officer see J. Colley,

J. Doyle, G. Logan, and W. Stettinious, *Corporate Governance* (New York: McGraw Hill, 2003). The impact of the composition of the board on corporate performance is studied by B. Baysinger and H. Butler, 'Corporate Governance and the Board of Directors: Performance Effects of Changes in Board Composition', *Journal of Law, Economics and Organization* 1 (1985), 116–17. A good introductory text to business ethics and corporate social responsibility is A. Crane and D. Matten, *Business Ethics: Managing Corporate Citizenship and Sustainability in the Age of Globalization* (Oxford: Oxford University Press, 2010). Principal–agent theory and stakeholder theory are also covered, respectively, by J. Stiglitz, 'Principal and Agent', in *The New Palgrave: A Dictionary of Economics* 3 (1987), 966–71; and T. Donaldson and L. Preston, 'The Stakeholder Theory of the Corporation: Concepts, Evidence, and Implications', *Academy of Management Review* 20 (1995), 65–91. The history of the Sentencing Commission's attempt to establish a code of business ethics is briefly told in L. Trevino, 'Creating the Ethical Organization', in *The Accountable Organization* (Westport, Conn.: Praeger Publishers, 2006). The grisly story of Enron is told by L. Fox, *Enron: The Rise and Fall* (Hoboken, NJ: John Wiley, 2003); and B. Mclean and P. Elkind, *The Smartest Guys in the Room: The Amazing Rise and Scandalous Fall of Enron* (London: Penguin Books, 2003).

Chapter 4: Public governance

The classic text of the reform movement in public governance remains D. Osborne and T. Gaebler, *Reinventing Government* (Reading, Mass.: Addison-Wesley, 1992). Useful studies of the reforms and their impact include M. Barzelay, *The New Public Management* (Berkeley and Los Angeles: University of California Press, 2001); and C. Pollitt and G. Bouckaert, *Public Management Reform: A Comparative Analysis* (Oxford: Oxford University Press, 2000). Sub-state developments are covered by L. Rose and B. Denters, *Comparing Local Governance: Trends and Developments* (Basingstoke: Palgrave Macmillan, 2005). For more recent work on network governance also see S. Osborne, ed., *The New Public Governance: Emerging Perspectives on the Theory and Practice of Public Governance* (London: Routledge, 2010). Much of the empirical work on the results of contracting out prison services in the USA is found in official reports and specialist academic journals. Books on the subject include J. Dilulio, *No Escape: The Future of American Corrections* (New York: Basic Books, 1991); and C. Logan,

Private Prisons: Pros and Cons (New York: Oxford University Press, 1990). The data on their cost-effectiveness is reviewed in T. Pratt and J. Maahs, 'Are Private Prisons more Cost-Effective than Public Prisons? A Meta-analysis of Evaluation Research Studies', *Crime and Delinquency* 45 (1999), 358–71. The implications of the new public governance for practitioners are discussed by P. Cooper, *Governing by Contract: Challenges and Opportunities for Public Managers* (Washington, DC: CQ Press, 2003); and J. and R. Denhardt, *The New Public Service: Serving, Not Steering* (Armonk, NY: M. E. Sharpe, 2007). On the changing nature of the state and how network governance operates in everyday practices see M. Bevir and R. Rhodes, *The State as Cultural Practice* (Oxford: Oxford University Press, 2010); the story of Mrs K is in chapter 9. The case for the continuing importance of the state is well made by S. Bell and A. Hindmoor, *Rethinking Governance: The Centrality of the State in Modern Society* (Cambridge: Cambridge University Press, 1999).

Chapter 5: Global governance

For a survey of realism, liberalism, and their competitors see S. Burchill et al., *Theories of International Relations* (Basingstoke: Palgrave Macmillan, 2009). One of the first academic texts to adopt the term 'global governance' was J. Rosenau, *Governance without Government: Systems of Rule in World Politics* (Los Angeles: Institute for Transnational Studies, 1987). Various perspectives on the analytic lens it provides are included in M. Hewson and T. Sinclair, eds., *Approaches to Global Governance* (Albany, NY: SUNY Press, 1999). Various perspectives on our changing world can be found in P. Diehl, ed., *The Politics of Global Governance: International Organizations in an Interdependent World* (Boulder, Colo.: Lynne Rienner, 2001). A useful study of the debates surrounding the idea of globalization is J. Scholte, *Globalization: A Critical Introduction* (Basingstoke: Palgrave Macmillan, 2005). On the impact of economic globalization on the role of the state see S. Strange, *The Retreat of the State: The Diffusion of Power in the World Economy* (Cambridge: Cambridge University Press, 1996). On the rise of transnational networks see A.-M. Slaughter, *A New World Order* (Princeton: Princeton University Press, 2005); and M. Warning, *Transnational Public Governance: Networks, Law, and Legitimacy* (Basingstoke: Palgrave Macmillan, 2009). For a positive assertion of the role of governance in development see F. Fukuyama, *State Building, Governance and World*

Order in the Twenty First Century (London: Profile Books, 2004). For more critical perspectives on 'good governance' as a development agenda see J. Demmers, A. Fernández, and B. Hogenboom, eds., *Good Governance in the Era of Global Neoliberalism: Conflict and Depolitisation in Latin America, Eastern Europe, Asia, and Africa* (New York: Routledge, 2004). For a participant's retrospective reflections on the landmines story see K. Anderson, 'The Ottawa Convention Banning Landmines, the Role of International Non-governmental Organizations and the Idea of International Civil Society', *European Journal of International Law* 11 (2009), 91–120.

Chapter 6: Good governance

Proposals for collaborative approaches emerged apart from the governance literature. One example is P. Healey, *Collaborative Planning: Shaping Places in Fragmented Societies* (London: Macmillan, 1997). Today the distinction between network governance and collaborative governance often remains unclear. Different perspectives include R. Agranoff and M. McGuire, *Collaborative Public Management: New Strategies for Local Governments* (Washington, DC: Georgetown University Press, 2003); C. Ansell, *Pragmatist Democracy: Evolutionary Learning as Public Philosophy* (Oxford: Oxford University Press, 2011); and J. Wondolleck and S. Yaffee, *Making Collaboration Work: Lessons from Innovations in Natural Resources Management* (Washington, DC: Island Press, 2000). On the democratic dilemmas posed by the new governance see B. Radin, *Challenging the Performance Movement: Accountability, Complexity, and Democratic Values* (Washington, DC: Georgetown University Press, 2006). For debates in development theory see B. Bull and D. McNeil, *Development Issues in Global Governance: Public–Private Partnerships and Market Multilateralism* (New York: Routledge, 2007). For an assessment of the Kerala Campaign see P. Heller, K. Harilal, and S. Chauduri, 'Building Local Democracy: Evaluating the Impact of Decentralization in Kerala, India', *World Development* 35 (2007), 626–48. The irrigation story is told by Wai Fung Lam, 'Institutional Design of Public Agencies and Coproduction: A Study of Irrigation Associations in Taiwan', *World Development* 24 (1996), 1039–54. For other visions and stories of empowerment through democratic governance see A. Fung and E. Wright, eds., *Deepening Democracy: Institutional Innovations in Empowered Participatory Governance* (London: Verso, 2003). On dialogic approaches to public policy see H. Wagenaar, *Meaning in Action: Interpretation and Dialogue in Policy Analysis* (Armonk, NY: M. E. Sharpe, 2011). And on participation in corporations see many of the essays in A. Wilkinson, P. Gollan, M. Marchington, and D. Lewin, eds., *The Oxford Handbook of Participation in Organizations* (Oxford: Oxford University Press, 2011).

Index

Governance

INTERNATIONAL RELATIONS
A Very Short Introduction
Paul Wilkinson

Of undoubtable relevance today, in a post-9-11 world of growing political tension and unease, this *Very Short Introduction* covers the topics essential to an understanding of modern international relations. Paul Wilkinson explains the theories and the practice that underlies the subject, and investigates issues ranging from foreign policy, arms control, and terrorism, to the environment and world poverty. He examines the role of organizations such as the United Nations and the European Union, as well as the influence of ethnic and religious movements and terrorist groups which also play a role in shaping the way states and governments interact. This up-to-date book is required reading for those seeking a new perspective to help untangle and decipher international events.

www.oup.com/vsi

Expand your collection of
VERY SHORT INTRODUCTIONS

THE AMERICAN PRESIDENCY

A Very Short Introduction

Charles O. Jones

This marvellously concise survey is packed with information about the presidency, some of it quite surprising. We learn, for example, that the Founders adopted the word "president" over "governor" and other alternatives because it suggested a light hand, as in one who presides, rather than rules. Indeed, the Constitutional Convention first agreed to a weak chief executive elected by congress for one seven-year term, later calling for independent election and separation of powers. Jones sheds much light on how assertive leaders, such as Andrew Jackson, Theodore Roosevelt, and FDR enhanced the power of the presidency, and illuminating how such factors as philosophy (Reagan's anti-Communist conservatism), the legacy of previous presidencies (Jimmy Carter following Watergate), relations with Congress, and the impact of outside events have all influenced presidential authority.

> "In this brief but timely book, a leading expert takes us back to the creation of the presidency and insightfully explains the challenges of executive leadership in a separated powers system."
>
> **George C. Edwards III, Distinguished Professor of Political Science, Texas A&M University**

THE UNITED NATIONS

A Very Short Introduction
Jussi M. Hanhimäki

With this much-needed introduction to the UN, Jussi Hanhimäki engages the current debate over the organization's effectiveness as he provides a clear understanding of how it was originally conceived, how it has come to its present form, and how it must confront new challenges in a rapidly changing world. After a brief history of the United Nations and its predecessor, the League of Nations, the author examines the UN's successes and failures as a guardian of international peace and security, as a promoter of human rights, as a protector of international law, and as an engineer of socio-economic development.

www.oup.com/vsi

THE U.S CONGRESS
A Very Short Introduction
Donald Richie

The world's most powerful national legislature, the U. S. Congress, remains hazy as an institution. This *Very Short Introduction* to Congress highlights the rules, precedents, and practices of the Senate and House of Representatives, and offers glimpses into their committees and floor proceedings to reveal the complex processes by which they enact legislation. In *The U.S. Congress*, Donald A. Ritchie, a congressional historian for more than thirty years, takes readers on a fascinating, behind-the-scenes tour of Capitol Hill-pointing out the key players, explaining their behaviour, and translating parliamentary language into plain English.

www.oup.com/vsi

SOCIAL MEDIA
Very Short Introduction

Join our community
www.oup.com/vsi

- Join us online at the official Very Short Introductions **Facebook** page.
- Access the thoughts and musings of our authors with our online **blog**.
- Sign up for our monthly **e-newsletter** to receive information on all new titles publishing that month.
- Browse the full range of Very Short Introductions online.
- Read **extracts** from the Introductions for free.
- Visit our library of **Reading Guides**. These guides, written by our expert authors will help you to question again, why you think what you think.
- If you are a teacher or lecturer you can order inspection copies quickly and simply via our website.